"I love Kerry and Chris. And I love this book. One of my deep desires is to invest the best part of me in those who are closest to me. This book will give you the inspiration and practical tools you need to do just that."

— MARK BATTERSON, pastor of National Community Church and author of *Primal, Wild Goose Chase,* and *In a Pit with a Lion on a Snowy Day*

"People are created for connection and community. We're each designed with a desire for knowledge and intimacy. But it doesn't just happen. It takes intentionality and a willingness to work. In *One Month to Love,* my good friends Kerry and Chris Shook reveal some practical and powerful steps that will help you cultivate your relationships. Whether you're seeking to strengthen your friendships or looking for ways to enrich your marriage, the tools in this book will help you experience the most out of every significant relationship in your life."

— ED YOUNG, pastor of Fellowship Church and author of *The Creative Marriage*

"Healthy relationships are essential for life, marriage, and family. *One Month to Love* provides counsel for developing a love that lasts and creating a legacy for generations to come."

— JACK GRAHAM, pastor of Prestonwood Baptist Church

"*One Month to Love* sheds new light on taking care of your relationships today. We have so many tools to help us communicate, yet so many relationships are in shambles. Chris and Kerry Shook give sound advice for putting those we love first and practical tips to make our love last."

— CRAIG GROESCHEL, pastor of LifeChurch.tv and author of *The Christian Atheist*

Praise for
One Month to Live

"If you want new urgency, fresh purpose, and a sharper focus for your life, then this book is for you. Read it and your future may be changed forever!"

—LEE STROBEL, author of *The Case for the Real Jesus*

"*One Month to Live* by Kerry and Chris Shook will add value to the life of every person who reads it. The questions asked and the 'Make It Count Moments' in the book will stir your soul and inspire you to begin, today, to make the rest of your life more meaningful. What Kerry and Chris present in *One Month to Live* could be life altering."

—KEN BLANCHARD, author of *The One Minute Manager*
    and *Know Can Do!*

"Regardless of where you are on your spiritual journey, *One Month to Live* will challenge you to passionately live the life you were made for and leave an eternal legacy."

—BILL HYBELS, best-selling author and senior pastor of
    Willow Creek Community Church

KERRY & CHRIS SHOOK

ONE MONTH TO *love*

30 Days to grow and deepen your closest relationships

WATERBROOK
PRESS

Previously released as *Love at Last Sight*

ONE MONTH TO LOVE
PUBLISHED BY WATERBROOK PRESS
12265 Oracle Boulevard, Suite 200
Colorado Springs, Colorado 80921

All Scripture quotations, unless otherwise indicated, are taken from the Holy Bible, New International Version®, NIV®. Copyright © 1973, 1978, 1984 by Biblica Inc.™ Used by permission of Zondervan. All rights reserved worldwide. www.zondervan.com. Scripture quotations marked (TLB) are taken from The Living Bible, copyright © 1971. Used by permission of Tyndale House Publishers Inc., Wheaton, Illinois 60189. All rights reserved. Scripture quotations marked (MSG) are taken from The Message by Eugene H. Peterson. Copyright © 1993, 1994, 1995, 1996, 2000, 2001, 2002. Used by permission of NavPress Publishing Group. All rights reserved. Scripture quotations marked (NASB) are taken from the New American Standard Bible®. © Copyright The Lockman Foundation 1960, 1962, 1963, 1968, 1971, 1972, 1973, 1975, 1977, 1995. Used by permission. (www.Lockman.org). Scripture quotations marked (NLT) are taken from the Holy Bible, New Living Translation, copyright © 1996. Used by permission of Tyndale House Publishers Inc., Wheaton, Illinois 60189. All rights reserved. Scripture quotations marked (Phillips) are taken from The New Testament in Modern English, Revised Edition © 1972 by J. B. Phillips. Copyright renewed © 1986, 1988 by Vera M. Phillips.

Italics in Scripture quotations reflect the authors' added emphasis.

ISBN 978-0-307-73097-8
ISBN 978-0-307-73208-8 (electronic)

Copyright © 2010 by Kerry and Chris Shook
Introduction and index copyright © 2012 by Kerry and Chris Shook

"The Paradoxical Commandments" are reprinted by permission of the author. © Copyright Kent M. Keith 1968, renewed 2001.

Cover design by Mark D. Ford

Previously published under the title *Love at Last Sight,* copyright © 2010 by Kerry and Chris Shook

Published in the United States by WaterBrook Multnomah, an imprint of the Crown Publishing Group, a division of Random House Inc., New York.

WATERBROOK and its deer colophon are registered trademarks of Random House Inc.

The Library of Congress cataloged the hardcover edition as follows:
Shook, Kerry.
  Love at last sight : thirty days to deepen and grow your closest relationships / Kerry and Chris Shook. — 1st ed.
     p. cm.
  Includes bibliographical references (p.   ).
  ISBN 978-1-4000-7380-1 — ISBN 978-0-307-45941-1 (electronic)
  1. Interpersonal relations—Religious aspects—Christianity. I. Shook, Chris. II. Title.
  BV4597.52.S56 2010
  248.8'44—dc22

                        2010018738

Printed in the United States of America
2012—Trade Paperback Edition

10 9 8 7 6 5 4 3 2 1

SPECIAL SALES
Most WaterBrook Multnomah books are available at special quantity discounts when purchased in bulk by corporations, organizations, and special-interest groups. Custom imprinting or excerpting can also be done to fit special needs. For information, please e-mail SpecialMarkets@WaterBrookMultnomah.com or call 1-800-603-7051.

We dedicate this book to all those who love us just the way we are:
our wonderful parents, our amazing children,
and a church that truly practices lasting love.

Contents

Week 3: THE ART OF RISKING AWKWARDNESS

Week 4: THE ART OF LETTING GO

A Personal Note to the Reader

What would you do if you knew you had only one month to live...one month to spend with the people you love the most? We have been humbled and honored to be a part of the lives of many for whom this question was not rhetorical. In fact, we wrote our first book, *One Month to Live: Thirty Days to a No-Regrets Life,* based on the observations we had made of people who knew they had only weeks or months to live.

One of the most significant observations was that people who know their time on earth is limited *immediately focus on relationships.* They quickly eliminate distractions that crowd out time with their loved ones and are intentional about letting those people know how deeply they love them. They don't focus on casual acquaintances; rather, they concentrate their time and energy on people with whom they have a *lasting love*—friends, spouses, children, parents, or siblings.

What if you found out that you had only one month left to *love*? Or what if you knew that the next time you saw a loved one it would be the last time? Are you satisfied with the relationship you currently have?

Because we believe most people would answer no to that last question, we wrote the book you hold in your hands. The thirty chapters in this book—one for each day of the next month—offer strategies and tools to help you live and love intentionally, to make those important relationships everything you want them to be.

After all, only by constantly aiming for a goal do we have a hope of reaching it. Intentionality, together with trust in God's power to do through us what we're too weak to do on our own, can help us achieve the lasting, loving relationships we long for. And when we fall short in our attempts to love as God does, we rely on God's grace to cover us.

As we did in our book *One Month to Live,* we have combined our two voices to be represented as one. These experiences and insights come from both of us, and rather than constantly identifying which of us is speaking in a particular section, we have written in the first person, as "I" and "we."

It's our hope and prayer that through this book you'll find the motivation and resources you need to make the most of the relationships that are dearest to you. We invite you now to turn the page and start the journey.

Kerry   *Chris*

The Most Important Thing

An Introduction

> Friendship is unnecessary, like philosophy, like art....
> It has no survival value; rather it is one of those things
> that give value to survival.
>
> C. S. LEWIS

> I don't wish to be everything to everyone, but I would
> like to be something to someone.
>
> JAVAN

Right now, there are three relationships in your life that trouble you. Perhaps a good friend said something to you yesterday. It felt critical, but you're not sure what she meant. The two of you used to be so close, but lately you've been drifting apart. Something's not right.

Oh, and your mother called. There's that. You know you should return her call, but you haven't. Why? You know there are things you should have said before, you avoided them, and now you feel it's too late. It's always so hard with her. Always messy.

And then...your son has been missing. Not missing physically, but he's been distant, quiet, silent. Missing emotionally. What's that about? What's going on in his life? You want to reach out, but he pushes you away. It worries you.

Maybe the relationships in your life aren't *exactly* like these, but I'm guessing these remind you of someone close to you, a problem relationship in your life right now. Maybe it's not your mother but your father, perhaps not your son but a daughter-in-law. It could be your best friend. Whoever it is, he or she is someone who matters to you—or else the relationship wouldn't trouble you, gnaw at you on the inside, make you question and grumble, or even bring you to tears.

I suggest you have at least three such relationships in your life right now that feel messy or troubling and make your heart ache a little. The number three isn't magic, of course. It could be just one or two, although it's likely to be more, not less. We all have relationships that aren't what we long for them to be.

Now I'm not talking about business acquaintances, casual or distant friends, fourth or fifth cousins. We all have a lot of relationships in our lives—maybe too many (and we'll talk about that)—but, quite frankly, not all are created equal. All people are important, but not every connection in your life has equal value. The relationships we want to help you with in this book probably include your husband or wife, possibly a boyfriend or girlfriend. Your mother or father could be on this list, or maybe a son or daughter. And there could be a friend, someone close to you with whom you've shared deep things.

It's these *meaningful, essential* people in your life—the *key* relationships you have right now—that we want to focus on.

So take a moment and think, who are these three key people in your life? Which meaningful relationships are troubling you? Relationships you wish were closer. Relationships you'd like to be deeper and richer. Relationships that trouble you, bother you, even make you a little crazy right now.

Seriously, think about it. Who are they? And now take a moment to name these three key relationships out loud.

THE HIDDEN ADVENTURE

The journey you're about to take over the next thirty days will help you improve, grow, and deepen those three relationships you just named.

I'm not saying it will fix everything (relationships aren't machines—you can't replace a broken part and be good to go). But if you apply what you read over the next thirty days, your key relationships will grow and deepen. Something will change for the better.

Trust me, this is important for you. In fact, this may be the most significant thing you do in your life right now. Why?

Because life is way too short. At the end of the day—at the end of The Day—in this all-too-short life we share, all that really matters is relationships. Our relationships with the God who created us and with the people we love. Compared to these relationships, the job or career goals we set now aren't really so important, the ladders we try to climb don't matter so much, and the objects we long to own and possess seem utterly trivial.

What really counts in the end is that special knowing look you share with your spouse, the arms of your child reaching up to you, or the quiet comfort of a friend who stands by your side in a difficult time.

The award-winning animated movie *Up* contains some profound truths about relationships. In a breathtaking sequence early in the film, we see the entire arc of the life of Carl, a balloon salesman, as he meets Ellie, falls in love, and gets married. They share a dream to travel to South America and save every penny for their big trip. But there's something familiar about the way their savings are constantly being used for the urgencies and emergencies of daily life. Before Carl and Ellie know it, they're in their seventies, and although they have a beautiful marriage, they never realized their dream adventure.

Ellie dies, and Carl is overwhelmed with regret about the trip they never took. In a desperate attempt to escape loneliness and recapture memories of

Ellie, Carl attaches a bunch of balloons to his house and sets out for South America!

You begin to realize as the movie progresses that this dream trip they were saving for, this object of their future plan together, wasn't really that important after all. The *real* adventure was the life they shared along the way.

The same is true for us: the adventure of a lifetime is right in front of us. It's just cleverly disguised as a familiar face.

Think about the possible loss of the relationship with one of those three people you named. You can't do anything about death and the physical departure of one of them from this earth. That's in God's hands.

But you can do something about your relationship with them in life.

UPSIDE DOWN

Much of what you've been told about relationships is upside down and wrong.

Researchers tell us that a baby sees everything upside down for the first few days of life until the brain can adjust the visual picture to right side up. Most relationships today are stuck in this same infant stage; we tend to see relationships upside down, and our culture only reinforces this view. The concept of love at *first* sight permeates our music, movies, television, and books. What we learn as children and continue to believe as adults is that a fairy-tale relationship somehow just happens.

Now, I'm not bashing romance, but meaningful relationships depend on seeing other people as they are and looking at them right side up. Real love— whether romantic love, a close friendship, or a family relationship—happens long after first sight. It shows up as people get to know each other more deeply and often after they work through tough things together. Real love in relationships isn't a magic act; it's a journey.

When people say, "It was love at first sight," what they really mean is "I was attracted to that person the first time I saw them." There is nothing wrong with being infatuated with someone at the start of a relationship. The real question, however, is, do you have a love that is growing stronger and deeper every day?

I don't believe in love at first sight; I believe in love at last sight. *Each of my relationships has the potential to be better the next time we're together than it was the previous time so that the last time we see each other on this earth we're closer than ever before.*

FRIEND ME

It's ironic that even though our society is more technologically connected than ever before, most people feel increasingly isolated and completely disconnected from deep and rewarding relationships. You can have hundreds of Facebook friends, but how many of them can you truly sit down with face to face and share your heart? It's more important to have one good friend than a thousand acquaintances.

Don't get me wrong: there's nothing wrong with social networking. Those sites can serve a useful purpose in connecting us to people. Technology is, after all, neutral. What matters is how you use it. A fire can burn you or warm you, and technology is no different. You can go online to research a medical question, pay your electric bill—or view pornography. The ability to connect with people online can be incredibly useful as long as you're smart about it, but it has its downside too.

The canary in the coal mine is this: social networking has changed our society's definition of *friend.* For instance, if I find someone named Joe online, all it takes is a simple right click, and my computer screen flashes a message assuring me that, yes, Joe and I are now friends. Hmm…now that we're friends, I wonder if Joe would drive me to the doctor when I'm too sick to drive myself or hold my hair back from the toilet when I'm throwing up. Should I count on him to help me out on moving day? Can I call him when my loyal dog has to be put down and I just can't do it alone? Will he tell me when I have spinach in my teeth, dandruff on my shirt, or my foot in my mouth?

We have bought into the false idea that if we're connected to huge numbers of people in cyberspace, we must be important and loved. There's nothing wrong with having lots of online friends as long as you realize that they're a random collection of people you might know or that someone you might know might know. A real friend is someone who is with you—present in your life—someone who gives you their time, shares your hurt, and feels your ache.

HOPE

Almost every day we hear about another high-profile marriage meltdown or a lifelong friendship falling apart. We look at the relational carnage around us and wonder, is it even *possible* to build a marriage that lasts? Is it *possible* to have a friendship that grows stronger through the inevitable misunderstandings and mistakes of two imperfect people? Is it *possible* to experience lasting love?

The answer is a resounding yes! The Bible says, "With God all things are possible" (Matthew 19:26). It doesn't say it's easy to build deep and rich relationships that stand the test of time, but we can say from personal experience that with God it's more than possible.

The two of us have been married for more than twenty-five years, and we can honestly say we're more in love today than ever before. We're two imperfect people who don't have it all together or figured out, but we've learned some principles from God's Word that have helped us develop a rich, unshakeable love for each other and for the most important people in our lives.

We want to share with you these lasting love principles that continually help us see life and the people we love right side up—from God's perspective.

First Glance

All relationships, whether a marriage, a family, or a friendship, go through the same three stages. This First Glance stage is often called the honeymoon phase, that blissful time when everything is sunshine and rainbows. It's the time in a dating relationship when you think you've finally met the perfect person, and all you can see is how alike you are. The honeymoon happens in family relationships too. But when children become self-thinking teenagers, parents and kids usually see one another's shortcomings more clearly. In a friendship the honeymoon begins when you think you've finally found a friend who really "gets" you.

There's nothing wrong with those first infatuated feelings unless you expect them to always be there. The First Glance stage is intense but fleeting, and trying to make it long-term isn't realistic or even desirable!

Second Look

At first everything seems beyond perfect, but then you take a second look. Suddenly you see reality staring back at you!

In a friendship, as you get to the Second Look stage, you see your friend's annoying habits and negative qualities. In marriage, that second look makes you realize that the person you're married to is not so perfect after all. Suddenly you're able to see only your glaring differences, and you start to wonder what you saw in them in the first place.

In the Second Look stage, you start asking, "What happened? Where did all the loving feelings go?" Nothing's actually wrong. Reality happened! And in a real way, it's good. Great relationships need to be based on reality—the true understanding and acceptance of another's faults, shortcomings, and weaknesses. This is also the stage where we admit we're not so hot either! It's in this honest acceptance of each other—acceptance of the real us, not the ideal first-glance us—that relationships begin to grow.

The danger of the Second Look stage is that it's easy to give up because we no longer have the sense of awe and wonder we had in the First Glance stage. Of the three key relationships you've named, is one possibly in this Second Look stage?

LASTING LOVE

Our goal is to help you get beyond the First Glance stage, which is by definition a shallow relationship, to move through the Second Look stage and not get stuck there, and to enter the Lasting Love stage, where the real work and reward of relationships occur.

The Lasting Love stage is the point at which you know each other's faults, fears, and true feelings, but your love is secure as you work to grow closer every day. Lasting love relationships are what this book is all about, and they always involve two people being honest, vulnerable, and feeling safe with each other. The reason you chose those unique three key relationships is precisely because you long for them to be lasting relationships. Maybe they're in the Second Look stage, and you recognize the need to move them into the Lasting Love stage. Possibly they're still in the First Glance stage, and now you're beginning to realize all that it will take to move them deeper. No matter what stage you're in or how long you've been there, the adventure of a lifetime awaits you in these pages.

LASTING LOVE RELATIONSHIP CHALLENGE

Practicing lasting love is a whole new way of living. These are not principles to memorize but an art form to learn and practice, and for each of the next four weeks, we'll focus on a new aspect.

Week 1: The Art of Being All There
Week 2: The Art of Acting Intentionally
Week 3: The Art of Risking Awkwardness
Week 4: The Art of Letting Go

I'd like you to join me in the Lasting Love Relationship Challenge. This book is the challenge, and you can do it on your own. Just read a chapter each day. There are thirty chapters, they're short, and you can probably read one a day pretty easily. At the end of each chapter you'll find the Lasting Love Relationship Challenge, which is designed to help you take the insights from that day and apply them to your key relationships. Also you can log on to onemonth tolove.com each day to access our personal coaching and get extra encouragement and advice or share your story. Our goal is to come alongside you to help you create the very best relationships possible. Let's get started!

LASTING LOVE RELATIONSHIP
Challenge

1. Get a small blank book to use as your relationship journal. Every day you'll conclude your reading with personal action points to record in your journal.

2. The Challenge starts with what you did just moments ago: in your journal write today's date, and list the three key relationships you want to focus on.

3. For the next month, commit one day a week to a Facebook fast. That's when you go a whole day without using social networking sites, limiting your use of technology to essential work or school-related work. Take the time you save to handwrite a letter to a friend or to meet a friend face to face for coffee. For more ideas go to onemonthtolove.com.

4. Think about inviting three or four friends to take the Lasting Love Relationship Challenge with you.

THE ART OF
BEING ALL THERE

Face to Face

Practicing the Art of Being All There

> To the world you may be just one person, but to one
> person you may be the world.
>
> BRANDI SNYDER

> For finally, we are as we love. It is love that measures
> our stature.
>
> WILLIAM SLOANE COFFIN

The first art of relationships is often the hardest: you really have to *be there* with someone.

By "be there," I mean really being with someone in mind, body, and spirit. The greatest gift you can give other people is your presence in their life. Offering your undivided attention to someone is hard, but it's absolutely necessary if you truly want to experience a lasting love relationship.

The number one problem in relationships today is that they usually take place at arm's length. We live in an age where it's common to live hundreds or even thousands of miles away from family and friends, yet technology enables us to connect almost effortlessly.

It's fun to post current pictures of the family or videos of the parade you and the kids went to this morning or the concert you and a friend attended last night. I'm grateful that technology enables us instantly to share the sights and sounds of our lives, but a quick e-mail or a picture shared on a Web page just isn't the same as being there. And in some ways, our increased technological abilities work to keep us physically apart. When we can touch a friend electronically, we don't feel as much need to touch them physically.

Our modern life and culture have led us to believe that relationships should come to us. We're used to calls coming in, message notifications popping up on our iPhone, and e-mails materializing in our inbox. In many ways our relationships seem to arrive at our doorstep, so to speak, and we end up managing the people in our lives through keystrokes and mouse clicks.

As a result, we develop the expectation that relationships ought to be as convenient as answering a text message or tapping Call Back on a cell phone. Gradually we're lulled into believing that creating and sustaining relationships should be easy.

I'll be honest with you: lasting love relationships require work and effort. Rich, rewarding relationships marked by love and respect cannot be developed and strengthened at arm's length. They require the commitment and tough work of finding ways to be there in person.

THE POWER OF BEING THERE

Why is physical presence important in relationships?

For one thing, just the effort it takes to show up in someone's life speaks volumes. Imagine that you're celebrating a birthday and one friend mails you a card, another drops off store-bought flowers, and another invites you to a special dinner and hands you a rare edition of a book you had talked about months ago. While you appreciate the kind thoughts of all your friends, you'll always remember the thoughtfulness of the friend who gave you the book. He's the one who invested thought and consideration as well as time and effort to make you feel special.

Likewise, our physical presence in someone's life means a lot more than a text message, e-mail, or phone call. The cost of friendship shown in the act of being there tells a person they are important to you. Most communication takes place nonverbally through facial expressions, body language, and tone of voice. So if you connect only by phone or e-mail, you're missing out on your biggest opportunities for getting closer. Technology can be a great side dish, but the real meat of a relationship ultimately requires your physical presence. Never underestimate the power of a hand on the shoulder or a warm hug; physical touch is powerful.

I remember an old story about Marilyn Monroe, memorable because it illustrates both how sad her life was and how meaningful one particular connection was to her.

Many years ago a freelance reporter for the *New York Times* was interviewing the actress. The reporter was aware of Marilyn's difficult past and how she had been shuffled from one foster home to another. The reporter asked her, "Did you ever feel loved by any of the foster families with whom you lived?"

"Once," Marilyn replied, "when I was about seven or eight. The woman I was living with was putting on makeup, and I was watching her. She was in a happy mood, so she reached over and patted my face with her rouge puff.... For that moment I felt loved by her."

Marilyn became very emotional when she remembered that moment. It was a playful, insignificant touch that probably meant nothing to the woman who gave it. But to a little girl starved for someone to be all there for her, it was an act of love she would never forget.[1] The power of that single physical touch was, out of a lifetime of experiences, still vivid in her mind.

The effort you make to connect physically says a lot, but another great reason to be there in person with the people you care about is that it creates a place for experiences to be shared. Sure, your friends can post pictures online of their trip to the zoo, their son's birthday party, or a graduation ceremony, but viewing snapshots and reading captions online simply aren't the same as being there and sharing the moment with them. Our lives are built on shared experiences, both good and bad—and there is simply no real substitute for doing life together.

The shared experiences of life bond us uniquely to each other. Being at the big game, spending time talking on the front porch, going to the concert in the park—each experience together is something the two of you alone share. It becomes just about your being with your friend or spouse or child and seeing and feeling something at the same time. That becomes part of your life experience and deepens the bond of your relationship.

WHAT IT DOES FOR THEM

I have a friend who is great at practicing the art of being all there. Several years ago his job required him to travel extensively, but he always did whatever it took to get home for the moments that meant a lot to his family. One particular time he flew to Hawaii to make a presentation to a major client and then flew back home the very next day.

I asked him, "Why didn't you stay a few days in paradise before you came back?"

He told me that his daughter had an event that he wanted to attend with her. Then he went on to say something simple and yet so profound that it has stuck with me ever since. He said his philosophy of life was "must be present in order to win."

I agree wholeheartedly. Being there in person for the people closest to us is the basic formula for successful, productive relationships.

When you choose to be all there for someone, you give them your most valuable possession: your time. Time is much more valuable than money, because you can lose money and make it back again. With time, however, once it's been spent, it is gone forever. So every minute you spend with someone in your life is adding tremendous value to the relationship. You are making a powerful statement that the relationship is worth your most valuable commodity.

In Hebrews 13:5 God says to us, "Never will I leave you; never will I forsake you." That verse is a powerful reminder to me of the value my Creator places on his relationship with me. God chooses to be all there for me no matter what I go through in life. God is never too busy. God is never preoccupied with something more important. He is always present and available.

One day several years ago when my son Steven was nine, he came into my office while I was working on a talk to give the next day. I was in the middle of a really busy week, and my schedule was overloaded with important meetings. But all Steven had on his mind was that I had promised to take him to get a trick yo-yo, which happened to be the big fad for boys in his grade.

At first I tried to think of a way to get out of it—I had so much to do— but I finally stopped everything, and Steven and I headed to the toy store and bought a couple of yo-yos. We got home, and Steven showed me YouTube videos of all these really cool tricks. We spent the rest of the day doing Around the World, Cat's Cradle, and Rock the Baby. I think I had even more fun than he did!

Looking back, I don't remember any of the big meetings that week, and I don't remember one sentence of the talk I gave the next day. But I will never forget the most important thing I did that week—being there with my son and playing with yo-yos.

WHAT IT DOES FOR US

Not only does our physical presence make other people realize that we value them, but the flip side is that being present with someone we cherish is meaningful to us too.

That's why we will do whatever it takes to attend the funeral of a loved one— even if it's out of state and we really can't afford the time or expense. We aren't doing it for the sake of the one who has already passed on. No, it's important for reasons we hold deep inside ourselves. We long to be present so we can acknowledge and internally memorialize the relationship we had together.

If we're willing to exert great effort for someone who has died, how much more should we be willing to do for the people close to us who are still very much alive?

Being There for Your Key Relationships

The point of each day's reading this week is to explore the art of being all there. It starts with physical presence—showing up in person to be with someone in their life experiences. The simple part of being all there is deciding to do it. The hard part is the cost of being there in terms of time, energy, and commitment.

Think about the three relationships you named yesterday. Hopefully, you wrote those names down in your relationship journal. Consider the personal cost to you of being present with each one of them. Are they worth it to you? Are they worth the cost of your time, energy, and commitment?

Love at first sight thinking says, "I'll wait until they show up for me. I'm too busy now. I'll just send an e-mail. If they're really my friend, they'll come to me."

Lasting love thinking says, "If I'm serious about making sure the people I love know how I feel about them, I need to take the initiative to get together with them."

This is the art of being all there.

LASTING LOVE RELATIONSHIP
Challenge

1. Consider each of your key relationships. When was the last time you were with each of them? Do you feel you've neglected being with any one of them lately?

2. Think back on an experience you had where someone's unexpected presence meant a lot to you. Write some notes reflecting on this in your journal.

3. Think about what sort of being-there connection you could make with one of your key relationships this week. Are you willing to do whatever it takes to spend some time together? Write your plan in your journal, and be specific.

Zoning In

Being All There in the Moment

> I love you for the smallest things; bluebells on my
> desk, a pat on the head when I make an awful speech,
> a cup of tea in the middle of a deadline panic, being
> the only one to tell me that the green skirt really does
> make me look like a sack of potatoes. And the big
> things; giving me the best things in your life, sharing
> my joys, being kind to me in all my failings and giving
> me courage.
>
> HELEN THOMSON

> Only through focus can you do world-class things, no
> matter how capable you are.
>
> BILL GATES

We all long to know that we're worth someone's total attention. That we're captivating enough or brilliant enough or talented enough to make someone stop everything else and, for just a moment, to be the only thing in their universe that matters.

When was the last time someone dropped everything they were doing and focused on you? When was the last time you felt like someone really listened to you—not just heard your words, but listened to your heart? Don't be discouraged if you have to think long and hard to remember the last time you felt completely accepted and unconditionally loved. It simply means you're like the rest of us.

HARD-WIRED

Children haven't yet learned to mask this insatiable desire to be loved, and they instinctively know if their parents are *really* paying attention to them. That's why as toddlers my kids would climb onto my lap, put a chubby little hand on either side of my face, and turn my head so I was looking straight into their bright eyes. They needed my full attention and weren't going to settle for anything less.

As kids grow, their pleas to be noticed shift from physically tugging on our hand or pant leg to verbal requests. Every parent has heard their child cry out, "Watch me, Mommy! Look at me, Daddy!" and then after the somersault or basketball goal or clarinet solo, "Did you see me? Were you watching?"

As children grow into their teenage years, we might not hear them call, "Watch me!" but the silent cry is still there. It's not just that they want you to acknowledge them; it's that they need to know they're *important to you.*

When we grow into adulthood, this desire to be noticed doesn't go away. It's hard-wired into us—the need for a relationship in which we *deeply matter* to someone else. So the question becomes, how can you meet this deep need in the people you love? It starts with undistracted focus—the act of being all there when you're physically present with someone—and it's an art that anyone can learn. The great news is, so few people bother to fully engage in relationships that, if you do, you will stand out like bright headlights on a foggy night.

IN THE MOMENT

"Wherever you are, be all there."

That statement has become a code in our family to remind us to focus all our attention on the moment we're living in. It sounds simple, but for me it's taken lots of practice to make it a way of life. My default state of mind seems to be worrying or zoning out, so I have to constantly and consciously remind myself to fully engage in every relationship that matters to me. That means that when someone I love is talking to me, I work to block out distractions and give them my complete attention so I can really connect with them. They need me to be all there so they'll realize I value them and believe they're *worth* my full focus. When I'm distracted, at best I miss out on what I need to know or understand about what they're telling me. In the worst scenario I'm communicating that they're literally not worth the time in my day.

Being all there isn't always easy, but it's also not complicated. For me, it takes just two steps. First, a conscious effort to clear my mind of outside distractions. Second, to step into the other person's world, which simply means to focus on what the other person's joy or need or hurt really is. I'm not even sure how conscious I am of those two steps, but they're there, and they seem to work.

You may be thinking, *Wow. There's no way I can stop what I'm doing every time someone talks to me.* Of course not. There are lots of people we deal with only on a surface level, like the neighbor down the street or the co-worker you pass in the elevator. You can't bring a high level of intensity to every relationship, nor would you want to. Again, we're talking about your key relationships: your spouse, your family, your closest friends.

Jesus provides a great example of how to fully live in the moment. When you think about his life, you have to be struck by the quality of his presence with others. The Bible tells story after story about Jesus in which he was clearly all there with the people he was close to. He was often surrounded by crowds, but he chose twelve people, his disciples, to pour his life into. Jesus knew that his biggest impact would come from the investment he made in their lives. He never missed an opportunity to teach and connect with them as they ate meals or walked through fields together. And because of the way Jesus connected with his disciples, they loved him and believed in him, and most of them ultimately died for him.

The truth of the matter is that being all there is not very *efficient*. If your definition of success is having your inbox cleared and your to-do list completed, then being there will feel harebrained and frustrating. If you're that Type A person who tries to make every minute and second of your waking hours productive, then the relationship work of stopping, focusing on another person, and giving them your time and attention will feel uncomfortable and even wasteful. But if you long for a friendship or marriage where you can share rich memories, secret dreams, and bellyaching laughter, you need to know that this is what it takes. Being fully focused in your relationships isn't efficient, but here's the great news: it's stunningly effective!

MULTITASKING VERSUS UNI-TASKING

The world tells us that if we want to get the most out of life, we need to get really good at doing lots of things simultaneously. So why not watch a ball game (relax) while preparing a presentation (work) and talking to your spouse about a big decision (connect)? You've just killed three birds with one stone, right? The problem is that, since you weren't focused, your spouse felt unimportant, your decision making wasn't as sharp as it could have been, and in the end you felt more stressed out than when you started.

Multitasking is a smart time-management strategy in lots of situations. I can drive while listening to a book on tape or run on the treadmill while watching the news. It makes sense to engage parts of my brain while I'm doing a routine activity. Running on a treadmill engages my body, but my mind is free to focus on the news. (And I love it when I get engrossed in a news story and then look down to see that a couple more miles have been logged.)

But the very thing that makes multitasking effective in some situations makes it destructive in relationships. That's because if I really want to connect with another person on a deep level, it takes 100 percent of my effort and awareness. To fully connect on a deep level in any relationship, I've found I have to *intentionally* choose to be there. To be *all* there.

My interaction with my family and friends becomes weak and superficial when bits of my gray matter get siphoned off to focus on other tasks. I'm just not that smart.

The Bible encourages us to be still and know that he is God (see Psalm 46:10). I think that's because when we're busy with the everyday details of life, we forget what's really important—we lose focus. If we live like we're speeding down a freeway, it's no wonder we miss the very things we were hoping to see along the way.

When our four children were young, every summer we took a family road trip. We'd pack everyone in with their toys, books, blankets, and snacks with the goal of driving as far as possible, as fast as possible, for as long as possible. Our plan was to make good time no matter what. One of our kids was prone to carsickness, and the only thing that could make us stop before the gas tank was on *E* was if someone yelled, "I'm going to throw up!"

Finally it dawned on us that we were blowing it. Our purpose in taking a trip in the first place was to enjoy each other. The goal wasn't really the destination; it was to grow closer as a family in a fun, relaxed way. When we realized how stupid we'd been, we decided that from then on we might not make good time, but we would make *a* good time. What a difference that made.

Where we were on the map didn't really matter as long as we loved who we were with. And that's become a picture of our lives, not just on vacations, but every day. Sure we still have goals, schedules, and plans, but they take a back-seat to focusing on rich, lifelong relationships. What good is it to arrive at your hotel on time but be so frustrated and angry that you're not speaking to each other?

And what's the advantage in racing through life and racking up awards, degrees, or deals if there is no one to celebrate with you in the end?

A GLORIOUS MESS

You see, rich relationships are messy. They don't line up in neat bullet points. They refuse to be boxed into a rigid schedule. They can't be filed for handy retrieval or condensed and expanded at will.

If you decide to invest in a heart-to-heart relationship, there will be times your eyes will sting with tears and your heart will feel like a vacuum-packed coffee bag. There will be times you feel the excitement of a kid in a candy store, times when you ache with regret or really burst with pride. But through it all, you will feel fully alive and fully loved. Author T. D. Jakes expresses it beautifully:

If you are looking for someone to be your everything, don't look around, look up! God is the only One who can be everything. By expecting perfection from the flesh, you ask more out of someone else than what you can provide yourself. To be married is to have a partner: someone who is not always there or always on target or always anything! On the other hand, should you ever get in trouble and you don't know who to look to for help, you can count on your partner! It is to have someone to curl up against when the world seems cold and life uncertain. It is having someone who is as concerned as you are when your children are ill. It is having a hand that keeps checking your forehead when you aren't well. To be married is to have someone's shoulder to cry on as they lower your parent's body into the ground. It is wrapping wrinkled knees in warm blankets and giggling without teeth! To the person you marry you are saying, "When my time comes to leave this world and the chill of eternity blows away my birthdays and my future stands still in the night; it's your face I want to kiss good-bye. It is your hand I want to squeeze as I slip from time into eternity. As the curtain closes on all I have attempted to do and be; I want to look into your eyes and see that I mattered. Not what I looked like. Not what I did or how much money I made. Not even how talented I was. I want to look into the teary eyes of someone who loved me and see; I mattered!"[2]

That ought to resonate with anyone who has a heartbeat. We all want to matter. The art of being all there starts with the unselfish act of taking what we ourselves long for and realizing that others want the same thing from us.

The people you love need to know they are important in your eyes. The best way to communicate that is to be present with them and focused on them, to clear your mind of distractions and dare to live fully in their world.

Try this: focus. When you're with someone you really care about, make them the most important person in your world. Just watch how this basic skill transforms your key relationships.

LASTING LOVE RELATIONSHIP
Challenge

1. Who have you known who made you feel like they were all there for you? How did their life impact yours? How can you do the same for the important people in your life?

2. The biggest reason most of us don't practice the art of being all there is that we're too busy worrying about getting our own need for attention met. How can you refocus your vision to see others' needs in spite of your own?

3. Try an experiment this week with one of your key relationships. When you're with them (in person), focus on them wholly, block out your own needs and worries, and consciously make them the most important person in your world. Afterward, write down your impressions of what happened as a result.

Invisible

Being All There on a Deeper Level

> I see her every day, and always for the first time.
>
> JEAN RACINE

> The question is not what you look at but what you see.
>
> HENRY DAVID THOREAU

Have you ever felt like you were invisible? Ever been talking to someone and realized they weren't really listening but were looking past you to see if someone more important was in the room?

I had an experience recently that made me feel completely invisible. I flew to Nashville to surprise my son Josh at his college. When I arrived, I made my way with my printed reservation to the rental car clerk. I handed over the reservation, and the clerk said, "Oh, we're sorry, but we gave away your car."

"What do you mean you gave away my car?" I replied. "I have a reservation!" He informed me that it was CMA (Country Music Awards) week, and they were really busy with lots of important people coming through. They didn't have any cars left, but I would get the next car that came in. He went on to say, "You just picked a really bad time to come to Nashville." I thought, *No, you picked a really bad time to give away my car.*

Then I stopped myself and thought, *Lord, what are you trying to teach me in this situation?* Well, two hours later when I still didn't have a car, a deep, profound spiritual truth came into my heart: *never use this rental car company again.* Eventually I managed to get a car from another company and finally got to my hotel. When I gave my reservation number to the lady behind the reception desk, she said, "We're so sorry, but we gave away your room." *Here we go again,* I thought. "It's because it's CMA week," the woman said, "and it's really busy." By that time I *really* felt invisible.

In time I found another hotel, unloaded my bags, and immediately left to drive to my son's house to surprise him. I drove up, parked, and walked to the front porch. There was Josh sitting with a friend. When he saw me, he yelled, "Wow! I can't believe you're here!" He ran to meet me and gave me the biggest hug. Finally I was no longer invisible. I was a VIP to my son.

Sadly, it's often the people closest to us that we treat as invisible. We sometimes look right at them but miss who they really are. We can be with them in person but gloss over their needs and concerns, failing to see what's underneath. Do you really see the people closest to you? I mean, do you *really see* them? Do you see their needs, their feelings, their dreams, their fears, their passions? Do you see their heart?

MAYBERRY MOMENT

Awhile back I was flipping through the channels and came across *The Andy Griffith Show* on one of the retro stations. It was the episode where a wealthy businessman from Charlotte by the name of Malcolm Tucker is on his way to the big city for an important meeting when his car breaks down just outside of Mayberry.

Tucker anxiously walks into town and meets Andy coming out of Sunday church. Andy listens to his predicament and tells him that they'll help any way they can, but he calmly explains it's really hard to get anything done on a Sunday in Mayberry. Tucker is frustrated and annoyed when he finds that the gas station is closed on Sunday and he can't get his car repaired. He can't stand Mayberry and wants to get on to his important business, yet he's stuck there. Irritated, he refuses to eat Sunday dinner with Andy and his family. He refuses to sit on the front porch and relax. Finally he loses it completely and screams out, "Everyone in Mayberry is living in another world!" (Which was true.)

After giving up all hope of his car being repaired, he resigns himself to the front porch, where he finds Andy and Barney, who's strumming a guitar. Only then does Tucker start to relax for the first time in a long time. He slowly begins to see the people of Mayberry—really see them—and what the true priorities in life should be.

Eventually Goober, the gas station guy, drives up in Tucker's car and says that he had some extra time on his hands and went ahead and fixed the car. He doesn't even charge for the work, saying, "It was just a clogged fuel pump." Tucker realizes that the very things that had frustrated him about Mayberry are the values he needs in his life. Now he's sad to leave.

How often are we like Tucker—speeding through life? To him, the people of Mayberry were invisible; all he had in sight were his urgencies. He had been blind to people.

Unfortunately, it sometimes takes a breakdown—of a car or a life—to refocus us on what's really important.

A Deeper Look

No one was invisible to Jesus Christ. He saw everyone, not just on the surface, but deep into their hearts.

Consider the story of Jesus and the woman at the well. The woman was a Samaritan, and Jesus was a Jew. The Bible tells us that Jews did not associate with Samaritans, but Jesus focused on hearts, not prejudices. Despite societal customs that surrounded their meeting, Jesus saw her heart.

He asked the woman to give him a drink. She replied by saying she wasn't worthy. Who was she, a Samaritan woman, to give him a drink? Jesus said to her, "If you knew the gift of God and who it is who asks you for a drink, you would have asked him and he would have given you living water" (John 4:10). She must have realized that Jesus had the power to save her, because she asked him for this living water.

Jesus then told her to get her husband and return to the well (he clearly knew a lot about the woman). The woman responded, "I have no husband." And Jesus replied to her, "The fact is, you have had five husbands, and the man you now have is not your husband" (verses 17–18). It was as if Jesus could see into her heart. And, of course, he could. The woman, the Bible says, came to believe that Jesus was indeed the long-awaited Messiah and eagerly told others about him.

Of course, Jesus is God, and we're not. We don't have divine powers to see into people's hearts. But in Jesus we have a model for relationships. He dismissed the distractions of society to notice and speak to the woman at the well. He perceived that what she claimed on the surface was not what truly rested deep in her heart. And the God of the universe chose to be all there for her.

We need to see people as Jesus did. Maybe there is someone at your workplace whom you see every day, but you've never *really seen* them. Maybe you see the same homeless man on your way to work every day, but you've never *really seen* him. Maybe there is a member of your family whom you see all the time, but you've never *really seen* them. Maybe you've taken someone for granted, looking past them and not really looking at them.

Maybe one or more of the three key relationships in your life have stagnated because you've been so obsessed with your own problems that you haven't stopped long enough to see the pain in the other person's eyes.

Maybe you haven't even taken the time with someone to share your own needs. One of the interesting things about the account of the woman at the well is that Jesus started it all by expressing his need: "I need a drink of water."

When you dare to express your own unseen needs, you tacitly give permission for others to do the same.

Above all, look below the surface of the people you love the most. Understand that what each of us presents publicly tends to mask what's going on deep down inside. If you really want to be a good friend, a true husband or wife, or a loving brother or daughter, you'll care enough to look and listen for what someone is wrestling with underneath.

No One Is Invisible

For more than twenty years Nelson Mandela was held captive in a tiny prison cell in South Africa and was treated as if he were invisible. He was elected that country's president in 1994 just as apartheid ended. As president, he made sure to greet those who served him just as he would welcome a head of state, remembering their names and genuinely asking how they were doing. Mandela had been treated as if he were invisible for so long that he never wanted anyone to feel invisible around him.

Stop today and take a second look at the people in your path. Start with the people you're closest to. You may be surprised when you stop seeing only what you want to see and begin to view them with new eyes and a sensitive heart. Let them know they'll never be invisible to you. If you do, when you see them for the last time on earth, you'll be closer than ever before.

LASTING LOVE RELATIONSHIP
Challenge

1. Spend some time alone thinking about the people you've named as your key relationships and reflecting on times you've been together recently. What was said? What wasn't said that might suggest a deeper need?

2. What things have you kept hidden inside yourself? Is there a revelation about yourself you're willing to share with someone you trust? Others will often open up if you do.

3. Take a second look at someone this week in your workplace, neighborhood, or school whom nobody (including you) really notices. How could you make that individual feel noticed and valuable?

Staying at the Table

Being All There During Conflict

True friends stab you in the front.

OSCAR WILDE

Avoid viewing conflict as a sign that there must be
something wrong with the relationship. Instead, view
conflict as an opportunity for growth.

WILL MOSIER

One of the most difficult times for me to practice the art of being there is in
the middle of conflict. It's my personality to try to avoid conflict if at all
possible. In the past when things got heated or emotional, I'd leave the room
or try to tune out everything.

A lot of people struggle with being there when tough issues are raised because they just don't want to deal with uncomfortable emotions. Many of us
have past experiences, sometimes from childhood, in which volatile emotions—
frustration, anger, and disapproval—created unsettling and uncomfortable feelings in us.

The bad news is that every time you suppress a tough issue in a relationship
in order to avoid conflict, you pay for it in the end. When you avoid or sidestep

real conflict with someone, the other person feels as if you're devaluing them. Avoidance eventually undermines the integrity of the whole relationship and keeps it on a superficial level. If you want to go to a new depth in relationships, it's essential to be willing to face difficult issues and stay engaged until you work through them.

THE PING-PONG METHOD

Communicating about tough issues is a lot like playing a game of Ping-Pong. In fact, table tennis is the perfect metaphor for two people staying at the table and hitting the conversation ball back and forth until they reach an understanding.

Many times when one person gets up the courage to talk about something that's really bothering them, the other person decides to ignore the problem and pretend everything's fine. When one spouse serves up a tough issue that really needs to be raised, their mate may choose the easy way out and let the ball drop.

Wouldn't it be incredibly frustrating if you were playing Ping-Pong, and every time you served, your opponent let the ball drop off the table and never hit it back? You really wouldn't have someone playing with you; the other person might as well not even be there. In the same way, nothing is more frustrating in a relationship than bringing up a difficult issue and the other person always letting the ball drop. The goal of communicating through conflict is to stay at the table, volleying back and forth and talking through the issue.

Another way we sometimes mishandle conflict is by slamming the ball and trying to force a quick conclusion to the argument. By playing this way, we're still not really participating in the game; we're simply using brute force to end the conflict quickly. This is a picture of not effectively being present with the other person and mutually working through a difficult issue. Keep in mind that the goal of conflict resolution in relationships is not to win the argument with slams and putdowns but rather to stay at the table and work through the conflict.

In our church we once actually played Ping-Pong together on stage during a talk on communicating in marriage. As we demonstrated the unproductive action of attacking each other rather than playing through the problem, we hit several balls at each other, and some ended up in the audience.

Several years later a married couple came up to me and said that they had saved one of those Ping-Pong balls and put it on the mantel to remind them to stay at the table during conflict. They also said they take the Ping-Pong ball down when one of them is frustrated and brings up a tough issue. "We have a rule that when you're holding the Ping-Pong ball, you have the floor and get to talk. When you don't have the ball, you have to be quiet and listen. We trade the ball back and forth until we feel like we've been heard and understood."

Maybe you need an object that helps you remember to stay at the table during conflict and really listen. (Just make sure it's not a sharp object! Ping-Pong balls are much safer.)

Tips for Staying at the Table

Careful beginnings. Consider starting with introductory questions such as, "Do we have a problem?" or, "Can we talk about something?" Sometimes the hardest thing in conflict is the beginning, the initial act of bringing up the issue. Often we set ourselves up for failure because the first words out of our mouths are negative or accusatory. If you begin with a simple, neutral question rather than a statement or an argumentative assertion (a Ping-Pong slam), the other person is more likely to engage with you. They'll sense that you want to connect with them, and most people will respond more positively to this than to an all-out attack. Remember, the goal is to improve your relationship, not kill it, and your opening words will reveal your motives.

Remember that most people are just like us in not wanting to face conflict. Dare to do the difficult work of staying at the table by initiating the conversation with, "Is there a problem we need to discuss?"

Shared feelings. "This is what I'm feeling. Do you feel the same way?" Those words can be so effective in conflict. The two of you may have a disagreement, but when you speak these words, you bond with the other person by discovering what you have in common—the distress, hurt, or frustration you both feel over the conflict. The issue may have you at odds, but likely the feelings from the conflict are something you share. When you ask, "Do you feel the same way?" you're including the other person on your side. You're inviting them in, underscoring that broken relationships hurt everyone involved.

It's important to remember that you really can't argue about a person's feelings. Someone can argue against your ideas or your beliefs or what you assert as fact. But no one can deny how you feel. So when you tell someone how you're feeling, usually it's quite disarming. It's an easy volley of the Ping-Pong ball. Often the other person will say, "I didn't mean for you to feel that way," and the door of communication will open a little further.

Real listening. The Bible says, "Everyone should be quick to listen, slow to speak and slow to become angry" (James 1:19). Usually we do just the opposite. We are quick to speak and get angry but slow to listen. Most of the time when we're in an argument, we hear what the other person is saying, but we're not really listening. To make progress in a conflict, we need to listen *beneath* the words.

Listening beneath the words is discerning what's really going on, realizing that what is being said is often only the top of a huge iceberg. If you're a parent, you've probably gotten good at this. You intuitively know that when your teenage daughter bursts into tears over something inconsequential, there's a deeper concern. It may be a hurtful comment a friend made at school or a longed-for boyfriend going out with another girl. If you're willing to dig in and discover the hidden truth behind her feelings, she'll realize that you really care about what's going on in her world.

Reflecting truth. So many arguments are based on impressions and exaggerations of what the other person actually thinks or feels or has said or done. Truth can easily get slammed in the Ping-Pong match of conflict.

Let's go back to the account of Jesus and the woman at the well. When she carefully chose the words "I have no husband," he saw the point of conflict she was avoiding. And he spoke directly to that, reflecting to her the truth of her life. Interesting that his first words emphasized a point of *agreement* between them: "You are right when you say you have no husband." He was saying that technically she was right. *Okay, we'll agree to that.* Then he spoke the actual truth: "The fact is, you have had five husbands, and the man you now have is not your husband. What you have just said is quite true" (John 4:17–18).

The woman at the well responded by saying, "I can see that you are a prophet" (verse 19). Interesting that she didn't deny what Jesus had said. Her response indicates respect for him. It's also not too much to assume from the account that she appreciated that Jesus didn't condemn her for having five husbands. She was likely called all kinds of names by the people around her. But this man Jesus spoke the truth in love.

Taking turns. This sounds so simple, yet it's rare in a heated conversation. Admittedly, it takes two to take turns. But at least, for starters, you can be the one to give the other person a chance to speak. Sometimes it works best to address this directly: "Okay," you might say, "we have different viewpoints on this. Let's take turns. You start. I want to hear your side of things."

One common mistake we make in taking turns is that while the other person is talking, we're busy composing our response. Often we're just trying to think of the next thing we're going to say or the winning slam we're going to make. Keep in mind it's not about winning; it's about improving the relationship. Too often we win the argument and lose the relationship.

Six words. "I'm sorry. Will you forgive me?" Those are tough words to say, and it's not appropriate to say them in every case. But sometimes we *are* wrong. Oftentimes we've inadvertently hurt another person, so an apology is warranted. But, yes, apologizing can be tough.

Understand this: apologizing is another way in which you show someone you love that you are there for them even through a difficult conflict and a tough request for forgiveness. And with those six words, more often than not, your relationship will be deepened, solidified, and made richer.

THE POWER OF WORKING THROUGH CONFLICT TOGETHER

When we were first married, we didn't bring up tough issues with each other until we were so frustrated and angry that we couldn't hold it in any longer. We learned the hard way that sweeping an issue under the rug magnifies the problem and creates bitterness. We've since learned it's better to bring it up right away. We serve it up and get it on the table before we get bitter, and we continue volleying back and forth even when everything inside us wants to walk away.

Sure, whenever one of us serves up honest feelings about something that's bothering us in the relationship, it causes conflict. The first few volleys can be pretty intense, because we feel like slamming the conversation ball at each other rather than staying at the table.

Over the years I've learned a lot about dealing with conflict in relationships. I'm still not great at it, but I'm improving. One thing I've learned is that there's power in the process. As we work through the steps of addressing a conflict, expressing hurts, listening back and forth—playing Ping-Pong—we create a shared experience that bonds the two of us. When we do, our relationship is stronger. We both realize we have the means to work things out together and face future conflicts.

The greatest joy you can ever experience in a relationship is the deep connection that comes only by working through conflict at any cost. Staying at the table is never fun, and many times it's painful. But it's really not about fun, is it? It's all about love.

Our culture says that conflict makes relationships too hard. That when there's a problem or disagreement, it means that the relationship wasn't meant to be, that you just weren't right for each other, and that it's time to move on. Lasting love says that conflict is a sign that a relationship is real. Relationships without conflict exist only on an artificial level. Lasting love says that two people working through conflict indicates that the relationship is worth something; it's literally worth fighting for. Remember, conflict is not necessarily a bad thing. The process of working through conflict enriches relationships and makes them more meaningful and authentic.

Being there through conflict and disagreement and hurt, staying at the table, is an important step in growing and deepening your key relationships. Watch what happens when you remain present in each other's life and work through tough conflicts together.

LASTING LOVE RELATIONSHIP
Challenge

1. When faced with conflict, do you get more emotional, or do you tend to withdraw? Think about how the people closest to you handle conflict. How do you address conflict with them?

2. Go online to onemonthtolove.com, and watch Kerry and Chris demonstrate the Ping-Pong method of being all there during conflict. Find a symbol to remind yourself to stay at the table the next time you're communicating through a difficult issue. You'll find some suggestions at onemonthtolove.com.

3. From one to ten (with ten being the highest), rate yourself on how well you really listen to the people in your life.

Stuck with Me

Being All There No Matter What

> The greatest happiness in life is the conviction that we
> are loved—loved for ourselves, or rather, loved in spite
> of ourselves.
>
> VICTOR HUGO

> If you're never scared or embarrassed or hurt, it means
> you never take any chances.
>
> JULIA SOREL

A by-product of sharing your life with someone is having your own "inside vocabulary," code phrases that communicate volumes of emotion in just a few words. In our marriage the phrase "You're stuck with me!" is packed with meaning. It's what we say to each other when we admit a mistake, ask for forgiveness, or find ourselves in the midst of an argument. "You're stuck with me" captures the essential premise of our relationship and reminds us both that we'd better figure out how to get along, because neither of us is going anywhere.

FRAMING YOUR RELATIONSHIPS

Our church has had an ongoing relief and rebuilding effort in Haiti ever since our hearts were moved, along with the rest of the world's, when we saw the devastation the people suffered after a 7.0 earthquake hit on January 12, 2010. More than 3 million people were affected when an entire city was pulverized during the initial event and ongoing aftershocks. An estimated 222,000 people lost their lives, largely due to insufficient and unregulated building codes. Shops and homes looked sturdy from the outside, but the buildings simply weren't built with an earthquake in mind.

In the same way, many close relationships appear warm and inviting: a bride and groom gazing at each other in candlelight, a new parent holding a cuddly, doe-eyed baby, or friends sharing hot coffee and laughter. It's easy to see why these emotional moments seem like they're enough to support a lifelong relationship. But the reality is that most of life is spent doing common, everyday stuff. Sure, great moments happen, but real life is lived in the midst of dirty dishes, overdue bills, and broken water heaters.

Good feelings aren't reliable enough to sustain any relationship. Here's the truth: our *commitment* to each other is the scaffolding that our key relationships are built on. Romance, shared dreams, laughter, memories, and deep conversations are the plaster and paint we use to decorate our relationships, but without commitment everything else will disintegrate with the little earthquakes that come into every life.

TILL DEATH DO US PART

Whenever I meet an elderly couple that has been married for fifty or sixty years, I have to ask them, "How did you do it? You must have weathered lots of tough times together over all these years—job changes, disappointments, health problems, parenting challenges, empty-nest readjustments, and times when money was scarce. But here you are. You beat the odds. What's your secret?"

The remarkable thing is that almost every couple responds in exactly the same way. They're quick to agree that, yes, life was very hard at times. Then they usually go on to share stories that make my eyes brim with tears as they tell of the heartbreak of losing a child, going to war, or struggling through an economic crash or natural disaster. This information is shared stoically, but they are always mindful of the original question and quickly move from the past to the present. Why are they still together?

Because they gave their word.

When they said, "Till death do us part," there was integrity in their promise. They've been held together by the *strength of their commitment.*

I'm used to this response now, but the first few times I was surprised. I had always assumed the standard answer would be "love." After all, if you can just work up enough loving feelings, your marriage can handle anything, right? No, I was dead wrong. The one thing these lifelong partnerships had in common was *commitment.*

Today's culture tells us that all we need is love. But in the end, love wasn't even enough to keep the Beatles together. It's ironic that a band that sang such great love songs ultimately had no love for each other. That's because love is more than just a song, a dream, or a feeling.

The commitments we make are like magnets: they pull us toward each other. In friendship, commitment means being there for someone even when it's not convenient. In family relationships, it's being by someone's side even after years of dealing with a disappointing father or a brother stuck in addiction. In marriage, commitment means that divorce isn't an option.

When you know you're stuck with someone for life, you'll do whatever it takes to resolve an argument. Of course, it takes two to make and keep a commitment, and if you've gone through the pain of alienation from a family member or a divorce, rest assured that God hurts with you and wants to heal your heart. However, there is no chance of lasting love in any relationship unless you begin with the foundation of commitment.

RECOMMITMENT

We've found that it's crucial to periodically recommit our loyalty to the people we love. Face to face, verbally. "I know you're my brother," you might say (*I'm stuck with you*), "but I also want you to know that regardless of whatever we've fought about before, I'm with you as you go through this."

In your marriage you might be tempted to think, *She already knows how I feel. If my feelings change, I'll let her know.* Well, it's time for your spouse to hear your words of commitment once again. It doesn't have to involve a special occasion or a candlelight dinner. Just take her hand, look her in the eyes, and let her know that you aren't going anywhere—she's *stuck with you!* (One important exception to this commitment, I strongly believe, is in the case of physical or emotional abuse or domestic violence. Those situations require professional help and sometimes immediate action for safety purposes.)

Becoming a parent carries the same kind of commitment as marriage. The "I do" is unspoken but is just as binding. In parenting, commitment means that you won't check out when your kids disappoint you; you'll stay engaged in their lives. It means telling your children time and again that there's nothing they could do that would make you love them any less or any more. You'll guide them, listen to them, discipline them, celebrate with them, learn with them, and pray for them…no matter what. You're committed for life, so you will do whatever it takes to reconnect with them. You see, in the end, you don't hold your commitments; your commitments hold you.

I remember getting stressed out when our children were younger and our days were incredibly hectic. Because I was determined to do the right thing in every parenting situation, it was easy to miss the unfolding joy of everyday life. My unrealistic to-do list and keen awareness of my own inadequacies to meet my children's deepest needs finally caused me to stop and think. As I reflected on my frustration, I realized that my commitment to the dream of what my family should be like was greater than my actual commitment to my spouse and kids themselves. That was my *aha!* moment.

I suddenly realized that, just like building a marriage, raising a family is messy. Of course! It involves imperfect people! That's when I began to celebrate the glorious mess of our family.

Suddenly I was much more focused on what really mattered—who my kids were becoming—and far less on the urgent but meaningless details and schedules that bombarded me every day. I was mildly surprised that the world kept turning even when we missed a baseball practice or didn't review for a spelling test. We traded high-maintenance carpet in the living room for dirt-colored, indestructible tile and installed a locker for each child by the back door so they could corral their own stuff. We used every tactic we could think of to reduce stress and create unscheduled chunks of time.

Here's the deal: your job as a parent is to work yourself out of a job. The process seems incredibly tedious most of the time, and progress is usually measured in months and years rather than hours and days. Sometimes it's easy to get discouraged and wish they'd just hurry and grow up. Many years ago I came across a piece by Erma Bombeck that captures the feelings well, and I have had it on my desk ever since. It concludes with...

Think about it. No more Christmas presents out of toothpicks and library paste. No more sloppy oatmeal kisses. No more tooth fairy. No giggles in the dark. No knees to heal, no responsibility.

Only a voice crying, "Why don't you grow up?" and the silence echoing, "I did."[3]

ENDING WELL

One of the biggest surprises of my life has been the rich, aching joy of having four kids who, along with my spouse, are my favorite people in the world.

Recently I took my youngest son, Steven, to a buffet-style restaurant. We slowly walked down the line filled with all kinds of mouth-watering choices, but when we got to the checkout stand, Steven's tray was still empty. He hadn't wanted to fill his plate with anything in case there was something better up ahead.

I'm afraid that many of us will be like this at the end of our lives. Sure, we may have racked up awards, accomplishments, and acquaintances, but a gold watch won't bring much comfort when it's time to leave this world. Chances are, even then we'll be striving to do one more thing, achieve one more goal, still trying to get our act together to prove ourselves. Meanwhile, we kept passing up relational opportunities in case something (or someone) better came along.

I'm so glad Jesus didn't wait until I got my act together to start loving me! The Bible tells us, "But God demonstrates his own love for us in this: While we were still sinners, Christ died for us" (Romans 5:8). Over and over, Scripture reminds us that God will never leave us. Likewise, we need to be there in commitment to the people close to us. Lasting love says, "I'll be there for you, no matter what," just as God is there for us.

No matter what.

LASTING LOVE RELATIONSHIP
Challenge

1. On a scale of one to five (one = get me out of here; five = you're stuck with me), how would you rate your commitment level in each of your key relationships?

2. What could you say or do to reinforce your commitment to the people who matter most to you so they'll feel more secure with you?

3. God stubbornly refuses to stop loving us when we are grumpy, arrogant, and sinful. He says we're "stuck with him"! How does your relationship with God affect the other relationships in your life?

Thick and Thin

Being All There in the Tough Times

It's so easy to fall in love but hard to find someone who
will catch you.

ANONYMOUS

There shall be such a oneness between you that when
one weeps, the other shall taste salt.

ANCIENT PROVERB

On a recent trip to California, we spent an amazing afternoon together, hiking in a forest of redwoods. The park rangers had displayed a cross section of one of these giants, revealing hundreds of years of growth. As we all were taught in school, the rings in the cross section of a tree trunk create a portrait of the life of the tree. With most trees each visible ring represents a year, specifically the transition from the late (dark) growth of a tree in the fall of one year contrasted with the early (pale) growth of a tree in the spring of the next year. By counting the rings of a tree, you can reliably calculate its age.

But the rings also show something of the character of a tree—its journey through drought and flood, hot and cold, light and darkness. A wide or thick ring indicates a season of good conditions. A thin ring represents a year of hardship.

In the same way, we go through seasons of thick and thin. In our journey through life, we all encounter both positive situations and negative conditions. Accompanying someone through the thick and thin seasons of life is what connects us to each other at a deep level. Great relationships are built on weathering the storms of life together.

On the one hand, this seems obvious. We need to stand by a friend's side when they are facing a hardship. On the other hand, culture conditions us to *limit* our commitment to others, depending on how convenient or easy it is to get involved.

Maybe you have good intentions to visit a friend who has been sick…but just not right now because today's schedule is already packed. Sure, it's important to visit your father at the hospital…but there's a meeting at the office, and you really ought to be there. He'll be up and around in no time anyway. Of course, you should call your sister who's been going through a tough time…but talking with her is so depressing, and you really can't deal with that today.

Culture tells us that commitment has its limits. Be there, sure, but don't let it cut into your lifestyle and margin of convenience. Lasting love understands that deep, rich relationships are built on being there *at all costs,* through thick and thin.

REDEEMING LOVE

One of the great stories in the Bible is that of Hosea and Gomer. Hosea was a prophet who was commanded by God to marry Gomer, a woman with a reputation of, let's say, questionable morals. Hosea knew this but married her anyway. At first they were happy together in marriage; it seemed to have started as a beautiful relationship. They had a son together named Jezreel, but Gomer's small family just couldn't compete with the allure of the fast and loose life she had been used to before marriage.

In time Gomer strayed from home and eventually committed adultery. She became pregnant and gave birth to a daughter. Eventually Gomer deserted Hosea entirely and went to live with another man. Soon her lover left her, and Gomer was impoverished and had to resort to selling herself into slavery.

Here's what makes this one of the greatest love stories of all time: *Hosea loved her anyway.* After she had deserted him, he searched for her. And eventually he found her—destitute, sick, dirty, and chained to an auction block, a shadow of the woman she'd once been.

Any one of us would have walked away. We would've said, "Yes, I was committed to her once, but look what she did to me! And she has ruined herself. I have every right to lead my own life now." But Hosea truly loved Gomer and was committed to restoring their relationship. He dug into his finances and pulled together enough money to buy her out of slavery. He literally redeemed her and brought her home as his wife once again.

The story of Hosea and Gomer effectively argues against all the excuses we tend to muster for those times when we feel inconvenienced, wronged, or even sinned against by others. It's also a model of commitment: being there for someone at all costs. The issue for Hosea was never "What's the limit of my commitment?" but "How can I save the person I love so much?" Not "When am I free to go?" but "How am I free to stay?"

The Bible makes it very clear that the story of Hosea and Gomer is symbolic of God's love and commitment to us. It's not only the story of the love Hosea felt for his wife, but it is also the divine story of God's redeeming love for you and me.

Love at first sight says, "I'll love you *until...*" Until you turn forty. Until you become too much trouble. Until I feel differently.

Lasting love says, "I'll love you *even when...*" Even when you're sick. Even when helping you is difficult for me. Even when your eyes dim and your skin sags. Even when you wrong me.

Can you say that about your key relationships? Can you say, "I'll love you with a Hosea love, with the love of Christ himself, *even when...*"?

REVERSE PSYCHOLOGY

One of the misconceptions we tend to have is that being there for a friend or loved one in need is about helping them get through a rough patch. It is that, but we often fail to grasp how much being there deepens and enriches *us*. We may think we're helping another "tree" to grow rings in the journey of their life, when in fact the rings being developed are in the tree of *our* life.

You may remember the beautiful film *Rain Man,* starring Tom Cruise and Dustin Hoffman. Cruise plays Charlie Babbitt, a self-interested twenty-something character. His wealthy father dies suddenly, leaving his fortune not to Charlie but to a mental institution that houses and cares for Charlie's autistic brother, Raymond.

Circumstances lead Charlie to take Ray on a cross-country road trip to meet with his attorneys. Charlie's intentions are selfish: to find a way to get some portion of their father's fortune.

But a funny thing happens on the way to the law firm. The self-centered Charlie begins to *understand* his brother, Ray. He begins to see life through Ray's autistic lens. The relationship starts with frustration and impatience on Charlie's part; he wants Ray to get better, to change, to improve. But through the course of the story, it is Charlie who is transformed. He begins to empathize with Ray and ultimately defends him against an intrusive psychiatrist. In the end Charlie has lost interest in the fortune and gained a relationship with his brother.

Love grows, like a ring on a tree.

Often as we make the effort to support a friend through thick and thin, the reverse happens: we are the ones who are helped. Being there for someone in the hard times of life is usually inconvenient and difficult and requires sacrifice. But often it also becomes its own reward, a privilege that gives back to us in unexpected ways.

Sometimes as we help others through a thin ring in their tree of life, the result is a thick ring in our own.

INEVITABLE

Thick and thin happen. Hard times—bad health, financial hardship, or emotional loss—are inevitable for the people you're close to. For you. For us all. It's not an issue of *if,* just *what* and *when.*

It might be worth thinking ahead. Consider your key relationships. If something catastrophic were to happen in one of their lives, how would you respond? How far would you go to be there for them?

Can you anticipate someone you love facing a health issue or personal crisis? What would you do? Sometimes the best way to help is simply to stand alongside and share in the need. If someone close to you is dealing with emotional stress or depression, will you muster the will and strength to sit with them through the down times?

True relationship is often defined by how you show up for friends and loved ones in times of deep need and crisis. These experiences shared between two people develop deep roots that will never be forgotten, often yielding unexpected rewards and blessings for years to come.

While you were instrumental in forming rings of survival in another's life tree, God was creating rings of growth in your own.

LASTING LOVE RELATIONSHIP
Challenge

1. Can you recall a time when you came to someone's aid and found yourself blessed in an unexpected way? Write down some notes in your journal as you reflect on that experience.
2. Can you imagine yourself having a "Hosea love" for anyone in your life? Who might that be?
3. Choose one of your key relationships, and try to anticipate a need they might have. If that need arose, what would you be willing to do in order to be there in the tough time they would be facing? Write that down in your journal.

Last to First

Being All There Before It's Too Late

Sometimes the shortest distance between two points
is a winding path walked arm in arm.
ROBERT BRAULT

Love between the very young is touching. Love
between the very old is glory.
PAM BROWN

A couple of years ago my friend Jimmy shared with me some bad news he had just received from his doctor. The cancer had returned, and the doctors had told Jimmy he had only six weeks to live. I was shocked and saddened, and giving him a big hug, I said, "Jimmy, I'm so sorry, but you know that everyone in the whole church will be praying for you."

I'll never forget Jimmy's response. I was blindsided with a powerful truth when he wistfully replied, "I appreciate your prayers so much, but really I need to pray for you and everyone in the church."

Jimmy went on to say, "I've been given a great gift. Now that the doctor has told me the news, I'm no longer distracted by life! My relationship with my wife is sweeter than ever, and I know exactly what God wants me to do with whatever time I have left on this earth. Everything is in complete focus for me now, but I'll pray for you—that you don't get distracted by life."

God gave Jimmy several months of undistracted and sacred life, and he left his family and friends with a blessed gift—and a prayer that I'll carry with me for the rest of my life. *I'll pray that you don't get distracted by life.*

As I'm trying to practice the art of being all there, it's easy for me to get distracted by the details of daily living. I put off the things that are most important and am drawn into the things that seem most urgent. I naturally drift into complacency in my relationships, as if my time on earth were unlimited and my opportunities to show love in this lifetime will never end.

THE LAST-TO-FIRST PRINCIPLE

Although I don't often think about it, I have a limited number of years, months, days, hours, minutes, and seconds on this earth...and the clock is ticking. When I admit the fact that my time on earth is limited, I have to acknowledge that my opportunities to love on earth are limited as well.

Embracing that truth—that my chances to show love are not always going to be there—makes me realize I need to say and do the most important things first.

Jesus said, "Many who are first will be last, and many who are last will be first" (Matthew 19:30). Christ was explaining that the pecking order in eternity won't be based on how the world measures success. Many people who are considered unimportant here on earth will have great importance in heaven.

When it comes to relationships, the last-to-first principle becomes all the more poignant. Jimmy's diagnosis made me realize how critical my interactions with him were during the brief remaining time I had with him on earth. Things needed to be said—the most important things.

The conversations we put off in our relationships are often the most important. One of the most powerful ways I've found to be all there for the people in my life is to ask myself, "What if I knew this was the last time I'd get to be with this person on earth? Would I say anything different? Would I do anything different? Do they know how much I love them?"

NOW IS THE TIME

John Maxwell, in his book *Today Matters,* says, "We exaggerate yesterday. We overestimate tomorrow. But we vastly underestimate today! When your mind is focused on yesterday, your heart will be filled with regret from the past. When your mind is focused on tomorrow, your heart will be filled with anxiety about the future. When your mind is focused on today, your heart will be filled with hope. If you change what you do today, your life will change!"

So why wait?

Why do we wait until the end of life to do and say the things that are most important? The Bible tells us, "Indeed, the 'right time' is now. Today is the day of salvation" (2 Corinthians 6:2, NLT).[4] The right time to be there is now, because now is the only opportunity we can be certain of. If you have something you need to say, say it now! If you have something you need to do, don't wait. Do it now! Love now!

I challenge you this week to say and do last things first with the people you're closest to, especially the three key relationships you have named.

In the movie *The Bucket List,* the character played by Jack Nicholson finds out he has only months to live. His bucket list consists of all the things he wants to do before he dies. Most items on the list are shallow and self-centered. And the movie is his journey through his remaining days as he does crazy, self-centered things: skydiving, racecar driving, and jetting all over the world. One of his bucket-list goals is to kiss the most beautiful girl in the world.

As he faces his mortality head-on, not much in his life can scare him anymore, except the terrifying prospect of reconciling with his adult daughter, whom he's been estranged from for several years.

He has never been so frightened in his life as he rings her doorbell and finally steps up to do what he should have done years before. As he enters the house, a little girl he has never met—his own granddaughter—hugs him. In that moment his list doesn't change, but he does.

And in the end he *did* kiss the most beautiful girl in the world!

LOVE AT LAST SIGHT

One sobering aspect of lasting love is this: when will your time with the people you love be the very last time you're with them?

Our time, their time—both are short. At the end of it all, we will be left with only relationships—with our husband or wife, family, and friends. And our relationship with the God who created us. Are you giving yourself to these precious relationships, or will you neglect them until it's too late?

As you live out the central principle of lasting love—how to make your key relationships better the next time you're together than they were the last time—realize that *this* time might really be *the very last time.*

I dare you to experience how this perspective can quite simply change everything.

LASTING LOVE RELATIONSHIP
Challenge

1. Many times the things we think are so important are really just distractions, and the things we perceive as distractions are in reality what matter most. Here's the litmus test: if it involves the people closest to you, it's not a distraction; it's what matters most. Journal about two or three things that routinely distract you from relationships.

2. Right now, schedule a time to be all there with each of your key relationships. Try to make this an in-person interaction. It may not be easy, but are they worth the effort?

3. This week focus on practicing the last-to-first principle discussed in this chapter. When you're with someone you love this week, ask yourself, *What if this is the last time we are together on this earth? Would I say or do anything differently?* Dare to let your words and actions be determined by your answer to that question.

THE ART OF ACTING INTENTIONALLY

The Imperfect Dance

Practicing the Art of Acting Intentionally

> There is no box made by God nor us but that the sides
> can be flattened out and the top blown off to make a
> dance floor on which to celebrate life.
>
> KENNETH CARAWAY

> There are always two choices. Two paths to take. One
> is easy. And its only reward is that it's easy.
>
> ANONYMOUS

A while back we took a dancing lesson together. I say *a* lesson because we quit after the first one! Let's just say that one of us was really gifted and with a little work could be on *Dancing with the Stars*. The other person was more...*choreographically challenged.* In fact, it wouldn't be inaccurate to use the word *extremely.* Yes, extremely choreographically challenged!

I'm always amazed at how professional dancers can make it look so easy as they move beautifully and effortlessly across a dance floor. Of course, great dancers will tell you that it took years of hard work, struggle, monotonous practices, and painful injuries to get to the point where it looks effortless and feels rewarding.

Isn't it like that with everything in life? To excel at anything—being a star ath-
lete, a super salesperson, or a professional dancer—you have to spend time on
the dance floor of difficulty before you experience the benefits of greatness.

DIVINE DANCING

So why do we think it will be any different when it comes to great relationships?

Upside-down thinking says that if two people are meant to be in relationship, everything will just click effortlessly, almost like magic. The problem is,
when you think this way, the moment the relationship hits the slightest bump
in the road, you start asking, "What's wrong? Why is this so hard?" Couples
begin to wonder if they married the wrong person. Parents are tempted to check
out during the difficult teenage years. Friendships start to drift apart at the first
sign of disagreements.

We have this vision in our minds of what perfect relationships should look
like, but when the tempo changes, we fall out of rhythm and stumble. And
that's when reality sets in.

At this point, we usually make one of two big mistakes.

Some people try to pretend that the misstep never took place. They just keep
dancing, hoping that by ignoring the mistake, the consequences will be erased.

Most people, however, start looking for another dance partner. They buy in
to the upside-down thinking that says great relationships should be effortless,
that the dance should happen easily, and that if everything isn't working perfectly, something must be wrong with the other person. If the dance requires
work, they conclude it just wasn't meant to be.

The right-side-up wisdom of the Bible challenges this mind-set. It teaches
that there is no such thing as a perfect relationship, because all relationships involve two imperfect people. Jesus told his disciples, "In this world you *will* have
trouble. But take heart! I have overcome the world" (John 16:33). Even though

we live in a broken and imperfect world, we can take heart because, with God's power, we can overcome even the toughest situation. Every relationship has its unique challenges, but it's how you respond in the hard times that determines whether you will walk off the dance floor in the middle of the song or discover the divine dance of lasting love.

ACTING INTENTIONALLY

The truth is that meaningful relationships take time, hard work, creativity, and most of all the art of acting intentionally. In fact, I would say that because rewarding relationships don't happen by accident, intentionality is even more important than chemistry.

We started practicing the art of acting intentionally in our closest relationships several years ago, and it has had an amazing, life-altering impact on our family. Early in our marriage, we usually had good *intentions*, but we were never very *intentional.* That is, we meant well, but we weren't focusing on our dance with each other. Failing to act intentionally slowly began to steal the passion in our marriage and the joy in our family. Our lives had become overcrowded and cluttered with things that felt urgent, but we were failing to be purposeful about what matters most. We found ourselves trying to please everyone, and it diverted our energy and commitment from the people we loved the most. Maybe you've experienced the same thing; you've run yourself ragged to please or impress people you don't even like, while the people you love slowly starve from your lack of attention.

We certainly don't have it all figured out, but we've definitely discovered that divine passion and joy come from following the path God has for us. We've learned that *we* have to decide what's important to us and spend our time accordingly. If we don't, there are plenty of folks who will be more than happy to plan our lives for us.

Mark Twain once noted that "a person who won't read has no advantage over one who can't read." How true. Just because I'm blessed enough to have a choice doesn't mean I'll choose wisely. There's a world of difference between *won't* and *can't,* but if I make poor decisions, the outcome will be the same.

Let's face it—meaningful relationships are optional. You get to choose whether or not you'll do what it takes to bond with the key people in your life. It's easy to place the blame for unsatisfying relationships squarely at the feet of the other person, and some or most of it may even be deserved. But never underestimate the power of choice: setting a relational goal and sticking with it can transform even the most dysfunctional relationship.

I Didn't Ask for This

Maybe you're thinking, *Easy for you to say. Clearly you've never met my mother!* Good point.

Here's the deal. Everyone is born into a family. There's been only one immaculate conception, and it wasn't you. We all have parents, and many of us have siblings, aunts, uncles, cousins, children, grandchildren, and maybe in-laws (or out-laws, as the case may be) that we collectively refer to as family. Let's be honest; you had absolutely no part in selecting these people to become a part of your life. You may even find yourself wondering what life would have been like if only you had someone else's dad or someone else's children. But the truth is, just because you didn't choose them, it doesn't mean they weren't chosen. God cherry-picked your family for you to draw you closer to him. And then *we* get to make the decision to invite a few key people into our lives, namely our spouse and some close friends.

Throughout our lives we're faced with a parade of changing faces: acquaintances disguised as influencers. First are grade school classmates, then a high school peer group, followed by college roommates, and work colleagues. The proximity of these people in our everyday lives makes us feel as if we should be micromanaging our relationships with them. We end up feeling stressed and inadequate, wondering why we can never seem to keep everyone happy at the same time.

The answer is simple. We were never meant to deeply connect with every person who wanders into our lives. Be kind to everyone? Absolutely. Constantly juggle scores of close relationships? No way. Even Jesus, although he preached and ministered to crowds, chose only twelve disciples to pour his life into.

The God who created us also created boundaries for our lives. Each day we're given a limited number of hours and a finite amount of energy. If you really want to experience lasting love, you need to come to terms with that fact and spend your precious resources of time, energy, and effort wisely.

That's the only way you can learn what real love is all about—the kind of outrageous love that will say no to a teenage daughter when saying yes would be less hassle. The kind of love that will choose a sleepless night rather than a warm bed in order to resolve an argument with a spouse. Maybe no one in your family has ever loved you like that. But then maybe, just maybe, that's why God gave you the family he did. *You're the one he wants to use to bless* them.

Choosing to engage in this kind of love isn't easy, instant, or painless, but it nourishes your soul in a way that countless acquaintances, one-night stands, and cyberfriends never will.

Many years ago I discovered a near-perfect description of what it feels like to be in this kind of all-out love relationship. If you've ever loved another person deeply, this passage from the children's book *The Velveteen Rabbit* by Margery Williams will resonate with you.

> The Skin Horse had lived longer in the nursery than any of the others. He was so old that his brown coat was bald in patches and showed the seams underneath, and most of the hairs in his tail had

been pulled out to string bead necklaces. He was wise, for he had seen a long succession of mechanical toys arrive to boast and swagger, and by-and-by break their mainsprings and pass away, and he knew that they were only toys, and would never turn into anything else. For nursery magic is very strange and wonderful, and only those playthings that are old and wise and experienced like the Skin Horse understand all about it.

"What is REAL?" asked the Rabbit one day, when they were lying side by side near the nursery fender, before Nana came to tidy the room. "Does it mean having things that buzz inside you and a stick-out handle?"

"Real isn't how you are made," said the Skin Horse. "It's a thing that happens to you. When a child loves you for a long, long time, not just to play with, but REALLY loves you, then you become Real."

"Does it hurt?" asked the Rabbit.

"Sometimes," said the Skin Horse, for he was always truthful. "When you are Real you don't mind being hurt."

"Does it happen all at once, like being wound up," he asked, "or bit by bit?"

"It doesn't happen all at once," said the Skin Horse. "You become. It takes a long time. That's why it doesn't happen often to people who break easily, or have sharp edges, or who have to be carefully kept. Generally, by the time you are Real, most of your hair has been loved off, and your eyes drop out and you get loose in the joints and very shabby. But these things don't matter at all, because once you are Real you can't be ugly, except to people who don't understand."

"I suppose you are real?" said the Rabbit. And then he wished he had not said it, for he thought the Skin Horse might be sensitive. But the Skin Horse only smiled.[5]

THROW YOUR HAT

In 1961 President John F. Kennedy declared that America had "tossed its cap over the wall of space" as he described his challenge to put a man on the moon and return him safely to earth by the end of the decade. It was a great analogy because even though the idea was grandiose and appealing, no one had any idea how to achieve it. Think about it. If you tossed a really nice hat over a really tall fence, chances are you'd be motivated to do whatever it took to retrieve it. Once the choice had been made to pursue a lunar landing, scientists all over the country mobilized to make the dream a reality.

When we purposefully choose someone to create a rich, lasting relationship with, we're throwing our hat over the fence. Instead of throwing our hat to the wind, we're announcing that this is the wall we've chosen to scale. Marriage is a choice. When you say yes to your spouse, you're saying no to every other person on the planet. Once you've invested your life in someone, you can't recapture those hours to use again on someone else.

BABY STEPS

If you want to infuse a weak or dysfunctional relationship with life, the key is to set small, incremental goals—something just out of reach that will require you to get outside your comfort zone. Maybe you had a falling-out with a parent or friend years ago, and there's been silence between you ever since. Even if *you* decide to do what you can to restore the relationship, the other person may need to thaw out slowly. Start with something simple. A letter is a good choice, because it gives the other person time to reflect on what you've said and doesn't require an instant response. A handwritten note will speak volumes more than an e-mail. It says you're taking this seriously, and you're already showing respect for the relationship and the person.

Depending on their response, or lack of one, you can choose what the next step toward reconciliation should be. Maybe a phone call or an invitation to meet for coffee if they live nearby. It's important to remember that there will most likely be difficulties on the path to restoration. Don't be surprised when hurt feelings surface or the other person doesn't seem to want to bury the hatchet. At times, being at peace with someone means knowing that you've done all you can to restore the relationship.

Intentional Versus Convenient

The act of intentionally choosing someone generates a huge amount of energy, hope, and joy. It's a catalyst that has the potential to ignite a lifelong, soul-deep relationship. When we go to someone and say, "Dance with me," and they take our hand, it creates great possibilities. It doesn't mean we're already skilled on the dance floor, but it does mean the two of us have chosen each other as partners to learn and grow with.

The connections you make with the people in your life may be intentional or convenient, but they're rarely both. Culture tells us that relationships need to be efficient, and if they're not, it's time to move on. This kind of upside-down thinking says that relationships just randomly come our way like traffic on a freeway, and we have no choice but to go with the flow.

Lasting love says that great relationships are based on active choices. The very best relationships are highly intentional, built on the solid rock of shared vision and goals.

The second art of relationships is beautifully simple but often forgotten in the rat race of our lives: You have to have a direction, a purpose, and sometimes even a plan for your key relationships. You must act with purpose, not just react to what happens.

This is the art of acting intentionally.

LASTING LOVE RELATIONSHIP
Challenge

1. Of all the people you know, list in your journal those you count as real friends. How many have you actively chosen to be your friend? How many are connections that have just happened to you?

2. Brainstorm a meaningful way you could let each of the important people in your life know that you've chosen them.

3. Write down some of the good intentions you've had for your key relationships that you've never acted on. This will help you get ready for the future assignment of writing down an intentional vision and action points for the relationships that matter most to you.

Painting a Vision

Intentionally Thinking Ahead

> Aim at heaven and you will get earth thrown in. Aim
> at earth and you get neither.
>
> C. S. LEWIS

> I used to spend my nights dreaming about the life I
> wanted to live. Now I live my dreams, and I spend my
> nights sleeping.
>
> DAN OGDEN

The most important part of acting intentionally is something we almost never do—that is, *paint a clear vision of what we want a relationship to become.*

To envision something better is rarely part of our thinking. People say, "I'll believe it when I see it." But God says, "You'll see it when you believe it," as in "We live by faith, not by sight" (2 Corinthians 5:7). Even though examples of true love are difficult to find, both in real life and in the media, you have to believe that something better is possible if you hope to achieve a lasting love relationship. That's why it's important to dream about what you want your key relationships to look like five years, ten years, or twenty years down the road.

Maybe right now it's hard for you to see past the problems and intense pain you're going through in a relationship. The struggle may be so great that you can't imagine any possibility of a bright future, and you're beginning to doubt that you'll ever experience divine joy again. King David in the Old Testament went through that exact experience. Because of his sins and failures, he was completely broken. David had been a man after God's own heart who at one time was so filled with joy that he literally danced before God (and before all Israel) with all his might (see 2 Samuel 6:14–15). In the thick fog of pain from his own mistakes, David couldn't see a bright future, and he may have even doubted that he would ever feel joy again. In his brokenness he turned to God and experienced forgiveness and healing. He said to God, "You have turned my mourning into joyful dancing. You have taken away my clothes of mourning and clothed me with joy" (Psalm 30:11, NLT).

Maybe you're in a time of mourning right now. Maybe you're despairing over one of your key relationships; you've been deeply hurt, and you're beginning to wonder if your heart will ever feel alive again. If that describes you, it's important to remember that difficulties in relationships are not only normal; they're also essential. It's the very problems and pain in your relationships that God uses to propel you to the destiny he has for you.

If you turn to God, he promises that your time of dancing is just around the corner. He can give you the power to see a clear vision of who you can be and what your relationships can become.

COLOR ON CANVAS

So how do you paint a vision for your key relationships?

As any artist will tell you, there's no one correct way to create a work of art. There are as many methods and techniques as there are artists. You have to discover the creative process that works best for you.

For me, that sometimes includes a list of prayers I have for one of my key relationships. Sometimes it is literally a picture I sketch. In other cases it's a goal or a set of goals I jot down. But usually it's a statement carefully crafted to reflect my vision for that relationship. The point is, at the end I have something that reflects my hopes and dreams for that relationship.

You probably need to start painting your vision on your own, apart from the other person. Spend some time reflecting on the relationship you have and then the relationship you wish for. If you are more visual, drawings or sketches might work well. If you are good with words, phrases and lists might be the best approach. The important thing is to get it down on paper so you can keep it as your private map for your key relationships.

At first you might feel a little intimidated by this assignment, and that's okay. Most of us aren't accustomed to thinking about relationships proactively; we simply aren't used to thinking ahead in a constructive way. But just imagine for a moment what might happen if you had a clear vision for what your marriage could become, or if you painted a picture of the longed-for relationship with your mother or father that so far has eluded you. Perhaps the dream you're putting colors and shapes to involves a friend. By painting your vision, you create a model for what the relationship might become. And from that model, ideas will surface as to how you can take concrete steps to make your dream a reality.

PAINTING TOGETHER

Eventually a vision for a relationship needs to be shared. One practical approach to this is suggested by psychologist Harville Hendrix in his book *Getting the Love You Want*. In short, you suggest to the other person that you each independently create a list of positive statements that you hope will eventually describe your relationship. Some of the entries, for example, might be

- We usually fight fairly.
- We enjoy walking together.

- We like laughing a lot.
- We are open with each other about what we like and don't like.

If you try this, you'll probably want to have a unique list for each of your most valuable relationships. Together, you can refer back to this list periodically to gauge your progress. The value of the exercise is that it gives you a reference point for ongoing discussions.

We've found that the best way for us to share our vision in marriage is to intentionally set aside a weekend at least once a year to recalibrate. So every year, around our wedding anniversary, we push everything else away and pull out our marriage vision. The great thing is that it's a living document; we can change and update it as we get older (and hopefully wiser). Over time it's really become the compass in our relationship. When we compare what our marriage *is* to what we *want it to be,* it's easy to see the midcourse corrections we need to make. Usually there are a few areas where we're right on target and batting a thousand and also some areas that have fallen off our radar and need some attention. That's incredibly valuable information if you're serious about experiencing lasting love. What's more, we've found that the very act of creating and sharing a vision for our marriage has strengthened it.

To help get your creative juices flowing, we want to share our vision statement for our marriage:

We are deeply committed and intentional about creating a marriage that is fresh and new every day. We feel completely connected to each other by listening and learning how to meet each other's needs so that the last time we see each other on this earth, we'll be more in love than ever before.

After you create an initial vision statement, the fun part begins: brainstorming together specific ways to achieve your shared goal.

Whether you use one of these techniques or create your own, the important thing is to become intentional about painting a vision for your key relationships.

LASTING LOVE RELATIONSHIP
Challenge

1. Begin to write a vision statement for each of your key relationships. Think about what you want your relationship to look like in five, ten, or twenty years. This may take several days, so don't rush it.

2. Pray for God to help you see what your relationships can become. He has the power to heal old wounds, restore broken bridges, and melt even the iciest heart.

3. For help with your vision or action steps, or to see our personal vision for our family and friendships, go to onemonthtolove.com.

Action Adventure

Intentionally Stepping Out

> We can do no great things, only small things with
> great love.
>
> MOTHER TERESA

> We love because it's the only true adventure.
>
> NIKKI GIOVANNI

We make sure that every Monday we go on a date. Having a "date day" helps us stay connected and keeps the romance alive in our marriage. Sometimes our date day includes going to a movie together. We don't always agree on the movie, because one of us prefers romantic comedies (guess who that is), while the other is more into action-adventure films. Unfortunately, the one thing we *always* agree on is the big tub of buttery popcorn that makes us feel sick afterward.

We really enjoy going to the movies, but we don't want to get in the habit of only going to the theater for our dates. There are two important reasons for this. First, we would gain about fifty pounds after a month of eating all that popcorn. The real reason, though, is that at the movies we can't engage in meaningful conversation. We wind up watching the adventure rather than living it.

First Corinthians 13 is often called the love chapter. There we see this powerful definition of real love: "Love is patient, love is kind. It does not envy, it does not boast, it is not proud. It is not rude, it is not self-seeking, it is not easily angered, it keeps no record of wrongs. Love does not delight in evil but rejoices with the truth" (1 Corinthians 13:4–6).

Every frame of this scripture shows us what love looks like when it is put into action. Love isn't really love unless it goes from the heart to the feet and becomes an action-packed adventure.

After you spend time writing a vision for each of your key relationships, you need to put feet on those visions. Focus your energy and create some adventures. To make this happen, you need to create an action plan. This isn't rocket science. You *can* do it. An action plan doesn't need to be formal or detailed, but it does require some time and dedicated thought.

Consider the main points of the vision you painted for your key relationships. Maybe one of them is to share hobbies, another is to laugh together, and another is to share the experience of traveling together. For each of those main vision points, consider two or three activities that might be possible for the two of you to do together. If one of you likes hiking and the other likes photography, you could plan a photo hike together. To create times to laugh together, you might plan to see a lighthearted movie together or even dust off some of your old home movies. If travel is your goal, you could choose a destination together and begin to research, plan, and save for a great trip.

If you have fallen into the habit of putting a lot of creativity and enthusiasm into your hobby or career and giving your family the leftovers, I challenge you to start putting the same amount of energy and creativity into your marriage and parenting as you give to your work. I'll bet you'll be amazed by how quickly things turn around and by how much fun you have in the process!

It's easy to get so caught up in our careers and social lives that we take for granted the very relationships we cherish the most. By intentionally crafting a vision and action plan, you'll have a road map that will help you arrive at your intended destination. Instead of being a blueprint for your miles, this map will guide your years.

OUT OF THE BOX

As you flesh out your vision, I encourage you to include some creative, out-of-the-box ideas in your plan.

When legendary comedian Jack Benny was a young man, he was very shy. The first time he saw Mary Livingstone, he was bowled over by her beauty. He desperately wanted to meet her, but he was too nervous, so he decided to have a florist deliver one long-stemmed red rose to her office. He did this for several days until she finally convinced the florist to tell her the name of the guy who kept sending her roses. The florist replied, "Well, it's a guy named Jack Benny, and he would like to take you on a date." Mary quickly agreed to go on a date with him, which marked the beginning of a wonderful relationship.

Every day of their courtship, Jack sent her one long-stemmed red rose.

Then they got married. After the wedding Mary thought, *Well, I guess the roses will stop now that we're married.* But to her surprise and joy, they didn't. Every single day of their married life, Jack sent Mary one long-stemmed red rose.

Then in December 1974, Jack Benny died. The very next day the doorbell rang, and Mary opened the door to find the familiar florist with the daily rose. Mary tearfully spoke of the passing of her husband and said, "So you can see, there's no need for you to bring the roses anymore."

To her surprise the florist said, "Oh, I know. But before he died, Mr. Benny made arrangements with me that I was to bring you one long-stemmed red rose every day for the rest of your life."

Now *that's* an out-of-the box, consistent, over-the-top way to express your love! We encourage you to put at least one crazy and creative action point in your plan. Far too many marriages slowly drift apart because each person was waiting for the other to make them feel treasured. Don't wait for your spouse to make the first move. You be the blessing. Don't try to outwait each other; strive to outlove and outgive each other.

Maybe some things you assume aren't possible really are. Don't let schedules, timing, or even finances discourage you from planning something extraordinary. If you try hard enough, you will discover creative ways of getting over the walls you think are limiting you.

DON'T FORGET THE LITTLE THINGS

Big gestures are impressive, but don't forget that most of the time it's the little things in your plan that will make the biggest impact.

A friend of mine decided that part of his parenting action plan would be to take lunch to his eight-year-old son at school. This dad told me that his son just beamed with excitement when he showed up. They ate lunch together in the school cafeteria, and then the young son grabbed his dad's hand as they walked back to the classroom. As this middle-aged businessman told me about this and the impact it had had on his son, tears filled his eyes. He said, "I had no idea that something so small could mean so much."

When my two oldest sons were in high school, one of the action points in my personal family plan was to meet them at their favorite restaurant every Thursday after school. I would show up early and be waiting for them with cheese fries and Cokes already on the table. This simple action took our relationship to a much deeper level over time. The smallest intentional action step can make all the difference in a relationship.

The most important thing to remember in planning activities to implement your vision is that they must be *steps into another person's world.* Many people want to be closer to someone in their life, but they're not willing to move out of their own comfort zone and into the other person's world to engage in something that person would enjoy.

Our son Josh is a tremendous musician, and one of the things he loves to do is go to guitar shops to check out vintage guitars. I really have no musical talent, but I'm crazy about Josh. That's why I love to step into his world and hang out at guitar stores.

One day we went into a shop and saw several guitars on the wall. Some were scratched, and all of them were extremely old. They looked worn and outdated to me, and I said, "Josh, those guitars on the wall look like they'd be pretty cheap."

He flipped over the price tag on one of them. It was eighty thousand dollars! Wow! Was I ever wrong.

I told Josh I thought the prices were insane, and I couldn't believe that an old guitar could be worth that much. Then he took one of them down, plugged it into an old amp, and began to play. Even I, who can't carry a tune, couldn't deny the incredible warm tone that filled the room. The sound was amazing and unattainable from newer guitars. I realized that every one of those expensive guitars was a classic instrument of exceptional worth.

Josh, the musician, had looked at the guitar and seen something valuable. He saw that in his hands it could make beautiful music. All I saw was a scratched-up, worn-out guitar. It was only when Josh began to play that I finally saw its value.

I'm so grateful that when God looks at us, he sees our value instantly. He saw past our scratches and scars and stepped into our world in the person of Jesus Christ. That was the greatest out-of-the-box action step ever! When I'm willing to move out of my comfort zone and intentionally step into someone else's world, it proves to them that I recognize their value.

Too many parents expect their teenagers to enter their world to connect with them. You can wait around forever, but that's just not going to happen. If I could, I would write this next sentence in neon and flashing lights.

If you want to connect with your teenagers, you have to look for ways to step into their world.

Get into their world. I've been to countless concerts and been nearly crushed in standing-room-only crowds right next to the stage, with my eardrums feeling like they were going to explode. And I loved it. I admit it's not my favorite music, but I love connecting with my kids.

I'm so glad God loved me enough to step into my world and care about the details of my life. I challenge you to follow his example and discover a whole new world by getting intentional with creative ways to express your love. After the first step, you'll never look back as you live out the greatest action adventure of all: a life of love!

LASTING LOVE RELATIONSHIP
Challenge

1. In your relationship journal, write out one or two action points for each of your vision statement elements for your key relationships. Think about what it will take to get into their world.

2. Consider an out-of-the-box action you could creatively introduce into one of those relationships. Realize that an idea is often followed by the thought, *I could never do that.* Really? Pray about it.

3. Reread 1 Corinthians 13, the love chapter, to refresh your memory about what real love looks like. Copy this chapter, the greatest description of love ever written, into your journal.

Crowded

Intentionally Creating Space

> It is easier to love humanity as a whole than to love
> one's neighbor.
>
> ERIC HOFFER

> There seems to be some perverse human characteristic
> that likes to make easy things difficult.
>
> WARREN BUFFETT

Some time-management gurus say, "You can get everything done by working smarter, working harder, and believing in yourself." I'm here to tell you just the opposite. No matter what skills, techniques, or systems you put in place, there never will be enough time for you to do *everything* you have on your plate. That's the truth, and it's freeing once you admit it.

You don't have time to do everything that everyone wants you to do, and you never will. But you do have time to get the most important things done. And the most important things in life aren't things. They're our closest relationships.

SPACE TO GROW

Our church has a farmer's field school in Maseno, Kenya, where experts teach local farmers smart agricultural practices to help them grow bountiful crops. This enables them to feed their families and lift themselves out of poverty. One of the biggest problems we've encountered is farmers trying to plant too many crops too close together, mistakenly thinking the more they plant in their field, the greater return they'll get.

We recently visited the farm of one man who attends this school, and together we strolled across his land. His amazing fields were bursting with row upon row of healthy, ripened cornstalks. As we walked, he explained how he used to plant his seeds as close together as he could, but the resulting stalks were puny and produced very little worth harvesting. He explained that he had since learned the principle of spacing, and now his harvest was several times larger. A little learning had a huge effect: his large family had plenty to eat with some leftover to sell at the market.

In the same way, most of us need to be schooled on relationships. We mistakenly believe that the more we crowd into our overloaded schedules, the more effective we'll be. But the truth is that growing relationships is a lot like growing crops; they need space to become strong and healthy.

The root of the problem is that our schedules are usually so crowded that the best things are choked out: rich and rewarding relationships. If you're going to achieve lasting love, it's essential to intentionally create space in your schedule for your key relationships.

Breaking out of an overcrowded lifestyle isn't just about time management; it's also about priority management. We have to constantly remind ourselves of what is most important in life. Whenever we find that our schedules are crowding out our close relationships, we ask ourselves a profound question that stops us in our tracks and gives us clarity on our priorities: What would I do if I knew I had only one month to live? Would I keep doing what I'm doing, or would I make some changes?

We wrote our first book, *One Month to Live: Thirty Days to a No-Regrets Life*, because we saw what an impact that drastic question had on our lives. We'd also had the privilege of walking with many people who were at the end of their life, some who had recently found out they had only weeks or months to live. We noticed a common thread: they immediately focused on relationships and quickly eliminated the nonessentials that normally crowded out their time with loved ones.

We started asking ourselves, If this is what happens when people find out their days are numbered, then why don't we start living this way now?

You probably have a lot more than one month to live. You will likely live for many more months and years, so why not learn how to really live *now*? Think about it. What would you do if you had only one month to live? Be ready to make some drastic changes if you seek to live with no regrets.

Lasting love takes this concept to another level. What if you knew that the next time you saw a loved one it would be the last time you *ever* saw them? How would that change your time with them? Would it motivate you to make more of an effort to spend time with them in an otherwise overcrowded schedule?

The Bible relates a story about Jesus teaching in the middle of a packed house. A group of men arrived carrying a paralyzed friend on a mat. They knew if they could just get him to Jesus, their friend could be healed. But they couldn't get close to Jesus because too many people had squeezed in.

Most of us would have said, "Sorry, buddy, we tried, but I guess today's just not your day." Yet these men refused to give up. Their steadfast determination to see their friend healed motivated them to come up with a creative solution. They carried the paralyzed man up to the roof and cut a hole through it, and then they gradually lowered their friend to the floor below—right at the feet of Jesus (see Luke 5:18–26).

Now that's a picture of a group of guys who had set a relational goal and would do whatever it took to reach it. Scripture goes on to say that when the paralyzed man showed up in front of Jesus, he was forgiven and healed. You see, when you realize that your time on earth is limited, you immediately understand what's important and what's not. That's exactly what happened to these men; they knew this was their last chance to get their friend to Jesus, so they refused to be discouraged and came up with a creative and extraordinary solution.

Can you imagine what creative and extraordinary things might happen if you brought this kind of urgent intentionality to the people closest to you?

REMOVE THE OBSTACLES

Once you realize what really matters in life, the next thing you have to do is act intentionally to remove the obstacles in your schedule that crowd out your relationships. Put simply, you need to decide what's important in your life and then cut everything else out.

Say you find yourself with a list of twenty things to do. They may all be worthwhile, but if you're really going to be focused on relationships, you probably need to cut that list down. So how do you decide? How do you prioritize and cull your endless list of to-dos?

The first practical change that really helped me was *learning to say no*. It's just too easy to say, "Yes, that sounds great. I'll try to do that," when I'm asked to attend an event or be involved in an activity. The problem is that in the moment, I usually neglect to think about the consequences my hasty decision will have on my relationships. Saying yes in the moment and allowing everyone else to schedule your life is ultimately a great motivator for change. It will drive you crazy!

Now that I'm ruthless in guarding my time, I've found it is sometimes necessary to pass up wonderful opportunities. But ultimately, the discomfort of disappointing some acquaintances and missing out on a few opportunities will never compare to the pain of regret I'll feel if I come to the end of my life and have missed the mark with the people I love.

Another practice that has been very helpful in our lives as well as in our marriage is getting together every week or two for recalibration. At least once a year, we do a big midcourse correction, but we've found that we need to constantly refocus together and be sure we're still headed in the same direction. Recalibration is when we sit down with our calendars and go over all the family events that need to go on the schedule first. We write down the open house at school and the ball games and band concerts. We schedule our date nights and our family getaways to the lake. We used to allow everyone else to fill up our calendar first, which made our most important relationships take the leftovers. Now we put first things first on our calendars by recalibrating our schedules with our most important values.

Do you feel that your schedule is constantly cluttered with things that aren't the most important to you? Someone once said, "We rarely change when we see the light, but we change when we feel the heat." So true. Don't let everyone else decide how you're going to spend your one and only life.

HOLY INTERRUPTIONS

Despite your very best efforts, things won't always go as planned. No matter how carefully you map out your days, things will inevitably come up and make life crazy and hectic.

We have to realize that when life interrupts, God has a purpose in it. I find that whenever I begin to forget that real fulfillment comes through deep relationships rather than accomplishments, God sends me a "holy interruption." Here's my definition of a holy interruption: God's greater purpose disguised as an annoying interruption to my man-made plan.

It's ironic that the things I think are distractions at the time are often the very things that are most important, and the things I think are most important are many times the real distractions. Interruptions are often divine appointments that God has planned for me. When I stop working on my writing long enough to pray with my son before he goes to bed. When at a moment's notice I interrupt my to-do list to help a friend move some old furniture. When I stop what I'm doing to call my spouse and say, "I just called to say that I love you and that I was thinking about you."

These "interruptions" are what actually matter most of all.

It's easy to forget that relationships aren't the distraction. The real distractions are everything else that keeps us from richly engaging with the people we love.

Learning to recognize holy interruptions can transform your relationships. The gospel of Matthew tells the story of some parents who brought their children to Jesus. Listen to the disciples' reaction: "Little children were brought to Jesus for him to place his hands on them and pray for them. But the disciples rebuked those who brought them. Jesus said, 'Let the little children come to me, and do not hinder them'" (19:13–14).

The disciples were completely distracted from what mattered most. They told everyone that Jesus didn't have time to waste on kids because he had important things to do and important people to see. Jesus, however, said, "Wait a minute! I'm not the one being distracted here. *You* are distracted. Nothing is more important to me than these children."

In order to act intentionally, you need to shift your priorities from things, accomplishments, and to-do lists and refocus your life on what matters most: relationships. Many times God will put an interruption in front of you—a holy interruption—which is his way of helping you see his priorities instead of yours.

The Bible says, "Be very careful, then, how you live—not as unwise but as wise, making the most of every opportunity" (Ephesians 5:15–16). Pray for God's wisdom to help you see the opportunities before you, and ask him to interrupt your schedule if he has something better for you to do.

LASTING LOVE RELATIONSHIP
Challenge

1. Do you feel like your key relationships are being crowded out by your overloaded schedule? What can you cut out immediately to create space for your relationships to grow?

2. What would you do differently if you knew you had only one month to live?

3. Is it difficult for you to say no to people and opportunities that come your way? Practice saying no as a first response this week until you are sure the opportunity is a priority.

4. Can you think of something in your life over the past few weeks that was a holy interruption? Write it down in your journal.

Games

Intentionally Going Beyond Surface Issues

> Oh the comfort—the inexpressible comfort of feeling
> *safe* with a person—having neither to weigh thoughts
> nor measure words, but pouring them all right out.
> DINAH MARIA MULOCK CRAIK

> Eros will have naked bodies; friendship naked
> personalities.
> C. S. LEWIS

A husband and wife were getting ready for a dinner party and were already running late when the wife said, "I've got to pick up a dress from the cleaners, and I can't find my car keys. I need to borrow yours." The husband was stressing out and replied sharply, "Okay, but hurry, or we're going to be late!"

Well, the wife got back from the cleaners, ran into the house, and changed clothes. Finally ready, the two of them dashed out to the driveway—only to discover she had locked the keys in the car!

At that point the husband lost it. He yelled, "How could God make you so beautiful and so stupid at the same time?"

Without hesitation the wife shot back, "Well, he made me beautiful so you would love me, and he made me stupid so I'd love you."

Our typical response in stressful situations is to point our finger at someone else, usually the one closest to us. It's one of many petty games that easily creep into relationships and cause a kind of relational paralysis.

In most conflicts, people argue about the same surface issues over and over again, never making progress toward resolution. If you really want to solve your relationship problems and experience lasting love, you have to be willing to get beyond the petty surface issues and intentionally go to a deeper level.

THE BLAME GAME

One great example of this is the very first relationship of all time: Adam and Eve. The first couple had the perfect marriage in the perfect place. Just think about it. No bills to pay, no kids to raise, and no in-laws. Not to mention they had no clothes to buy. Everything you need for a perfect marriage.

But then sin entered the relationship. And with the sin came the petty games.

The blame game was the first destructive game Adam and Eve played. Adam told God, "The woman you put here with me—it's her fault. She gave me some fruit from the tree, and I ate it" (see Genesis 3:12). Eve then shifted the blame and said, "The serpent deceived me, and I ate" (verse 13). So the very first couple played the blame game, and people ever since have been pointing their fingers at each other rather than dealing with the deeper issues.

The two of us have noticed over time that we're most vulnerable to playing the blame game when our stress levels are high. When we begin to feel overwhelmed in our busy lives, we begin looking to each other to lighten our load. When we both feel overwhelmed, we start taking out our stress on each other—and that's the most unproductive thing we can do.

Over the years we have slowly been learning to stop *taking* it out on each other and start *talking* it out with each other. Playing the blame game only adds stress, but talking about the deeper issues leads to real solutions.

HIDE-AND-SEEK

Another game Adam and Eve played was hide-and-seek. After they sinned, the great cover-up started.

They used fig leaves to cover themselves physically, but more important, they tried to cover up their faults and insecurities *relationally.* The fig leaves were really a symbol of separation, distance, and loss of intimacy. When we play hide-and-seek, our relationships are kept at a surface level, and we push the other person away.

Adam and Eve even played hide-and-seek with God. He called out to Adam, "Where are you?" Adam answered, "I was afraid because I was naked; so I hid" (3:9–10). It's ironic that they tried to hide their sin and guilt from the God who created them and knew everything about them.

Fear, however, causes us to do some crazy and unproductive things that destroy intimacy. It's fear that starts the hide-and-seek games, and our greatest fear is the fear of rejection.

When you first enter a relationship, it's easy to pretend to be someone you're not, but eventually your true self has to come through. You can't keep your actual feelings and character flaws hidden forever. The only way to really reach a place of depth and intimacy in a relationship is to risk baring your soul—the good, the bad, and the ugly.

God took the greatest risk of all when he created us. The Bible says God created you as an object of his love, and he desires you to love him in return. Have you ever stopped to think about that? The God of the universe, who is holy and perfect and needs nothing, gave us the power to choose whether or not we would love him back. He could have programmed us to do the right thing and love him in return, but instead he gave us the power to reject him.

Why? Because, *love isn't love unless it risks rejection.* Love isn't really love unless we stop playing hide-and-seek and risk rejection by revealing our true selves.

MONOPOLY

After sin entered the relationship, Adam and Eve also played the game of Monopoly; they struggled for control.

In Genesis 3:16, God said, "Your desire will be for your husband, and he will rule over you." Insecurity and fear changed God's perfect plan. Instead of husbands and wives working together as a unified team, sin forced husbands and wives to compete with each other.

The Monopoly game stems from insecurity. The more insecure I am, the more I insist on getting my way. Insecurity demands that I win every argument (to bolster my low self-esteem with a false sense of control and power). Many spouses always try to win the argument, and all the while they're losing the relationship.

GAMES PEOPLE PLAY

Whether in marriage, friendships, or family relationships, the games we play sabotage secure relationships. To grow closer, we have to get beyond the surface games and deal with the root causes of relationship conflict.

It takes courage to stop playing games and decide, I'm going to be honest from now on. I'm not going to act defensively, I won't deflect my responsibility, and I'm going to risk being who I really am in front of this person who means so much to me. If you intend to go deeper in a relationship, then you first have to get to the place where you quickly identify surface games when they appear. One dead giveaway that games are being played is if you never disagree on anything. When two people agree on everything, somebody is not being honest. When everyone on a team at work always agrees on everything, some people aren't sharing their true feelings. It could be out of fear of a reprimand or a desire to win brownie points, but either way it's a dysfunctional and dishonest game.

We've discovered that the only way to move beyond this is to create a safe zone where people can share their true feelings without fear. In our management team meetings at church, we intentionally try to create an environment where, behind closed doors, we can disagree, argue honestly, and express angry feelings. We've discovered that this promotes unity and commitment because after everyone feels their opinion has been heard, the respect level rises. We can then walk out of the room as a unified team, committed to the decision that was made.

If you feel an important relationship in your life is stuck on the surface level of being afraid to share negative feelings, it's critical to have an intentional conversation. I have a dear friend and mentor whom I greatly respect. We get together frequently to encourage each other, and I've learned a lot from his leadership experience. Several years ago we sat down over coffee, and he said something that took our friendship to a deeper level. He said, "I know you value our friendship, but you never tell me anything negative. You only say positive, encouraging things to me. There must be times when I do things that bother you. I want our friendship to go to a deeper level, and I want you to feel free to tell me when you disagree or don't like the direction I'm going in some area of my life."

I told him, "I respect you so much, and the things we disagree on are so minor, that I thought it would be unloving to point them out."

"No, it's just the opposite," he said. "I need your encouragement and your accountability, and it's unloving not to be totally honest." By intentionally creating a safe zone, we now feel free to be honest about both our successes and our shortcomings. And it's brought our friendship to a whole new level.

POWER STRUGGLE

Another sign that a relationship is stuck on a surface level is when there is constant arguing. When there is never any disagreement, there is not complete honesty, but when there is always disagreement, there is a power struggle.

The biggest problem with a power struggle is that it creates bitterness and hurt feelings without any breakthroughs. You may be attacking each other, but you're not really attacking the deeper issues that are causing the conflict.

To break out of a power struggle, I first have to take a deeper look at myself. When I play the blame game, it keeps me from identifying and taking responsibility for my part of the problem. Whenever I have a conflict with someone I'm close to, it's easy to see their part in the problem, but it's much more difficult to identify my part. That's because all power struggles involve two people who are acting selfishly. When I'm acting in selfishness, I can't see myself clearly.

It's important to ask God to help you see the selfishness in your heart that's contributing to the problem. Even if the other person is responsible for 90 percent of the conflict, you still have to take responsibility for your 10 percent if you want to make progress.

Then you need to take a closer look at yourself and identify the deeper cause of the argument. Is it insecurity? hurt? fear of rejection? frustration because you're tired or overwhelmed?

Once you identify the root cause, initiate a conversation that starts on this deeper level instead of the surface argument. For example, say, "When you do that, I have to admit that I feel very insecure," or, "I feel frustrated, and I know I express it in the wrong way," or, "When you say things like that, I feel hurt."

I'm not saying that you won't ever have conflict again or that you will solve all your biggest problems overnight, but at least you will make progress by dealing with the deeper issues. It takes intentional and continual work to grow a deep relationship, but the rewards make it all worthwhile.

ATMOSPHERE OF ACCEPTANCE

The most important step in getting beyond petty games is to intentionally create an atmosphere of acceptance. The Bible says, "Accept one another, then, just as Christ accepted you, in order to bring praise to God" (Romans 15:7). You will never completely understand or totally agree with the people you're relating to, because we all come at life from different perspectives. You can, however, create an atmosphere of acceptance where you both feel free to share your true feelings and express yourself without the fear of rejection.

Before sin and surface games entered Adam and Eve's relationship, "the man and his wife were both naked, and they felt no shame" (Genesis 2:25). I believe this is talking about so much more than physical nakedness. They experienced total acceptance. Their emotions and true feelings were totally exposed, and yet they felt completely accepted.

That's the deepest longing of every human heart: to feel total acceptance and the freedom to be one's true self. Lasting love means you move beyond the games and get to the place where you uncover your fears, your mistakes and weaknesses, your deepest dreams, and all your hopes in an atmosphere of acceptance.

LASTING LOVE RELATIONSHIP
Challenge

1. Which one of the surface games do you tend to play the most? Do you share your true self in your close relationships, or are you staying on the surface level?

2. Ask God to help you see the deeper issues that are affecting your key relationships. Write down one or two things you plan to do to get intentional about understanding the people you love the most.

3. If you have a relationship that is stuck on the surface, plan a face-to-face conversation, and begin the discussion with the root issue of hurt, insecurity, or frustration.

4. Go to onemonthtolove.com to hear Kerry and Chris talk about their differences and how they are learning to accept and appreciate each other.

In Between

Intentionally Getting Unstuck

> You formed us for yourself, and our hearts are restless
> till they find their rest in you.
>
> ST. AUGUSTINE

> If you are going through hell, keep going.
>
> WINSTON CHURCHILL

Have you ever felt in between? In between jobs? In between taking a medical test and getting the results? In between starting a big project and seeing results? Or in between where you used to be and where you want to be in life?

The truth is that much of life is lived in the in-between. Including relationships.

You might have seen a movie a few years ago called *The Terminal*. Tom Hanks plays an Eastern European traveler named Viktor Navorski, who passes through JFK Airport in New York. As he lands there, the government in his home country is overthrown, and Navorski's visa is denied. In short, he no longer has a country to go back to or the legal paperwork to allow him to travel anywhere else. He winds up stuck in the airport—not for hours but for months—and he effectively takes up residence in the terminal. The movie is a funny and sometimes poignant parable of modern life and the state of being in between.

In-between is a time of life when we seem to be on hold. It's a period of waiting, although what makes it hard is that often we aren't sure what we're waiting for. It's frequently tied to transitions as we change jobs, experience a health issue, or enter a new stage of life. In the in-between, nothing feels solid or sure, and we want to know what's coming next.

WHEN THE IN-BETWEEN IS GOOD

Are one or more of your key relationships stuck in the in-between? If so, the challenge is to discern if this is a necessary stage of life or a point of paralysis.

Virtually every hero of the Bible had to endure the place of in-between. Abraham's place of in-between was infertility. God had promised him that he would be the father of a great nation, and yet he and his wife, Sarah, had no children. Joseph's place of in-between was in a prison cell. He had a dream to save his family and an entire nation from a famine, but he was sold into slavery, accused of a crime he didn't commit, and thrown into prison for years. Noah's place of in-between was a construction project that seemed like it would never get finished. God called him to build the ark, and he worked on it for years with no sign of rain, just signs of rejection and ridicule from his neighbors. Daniel's place of in-between was the lions' den. Mary's place of in-between was pregnancy. Being unwed and with child by the Holy Spirit, she endured scorn and disapproval from her neighbors and risked rejection from her fiancé, Joseph.

Even Jesus experienced a time of in-between. He came to save the world, yet he lived the first thirty years of his life in obscurity until he performed his first miracle and began his ministry.

Clearly, the in-between times of life are challenging. They often include a learning curve, a real-life education that prepares us for our future. The in-between can also be where we experience God the most. It's where he gets our attention, which often results in change, maturity, growth, and a deeper faith. Faith is forged in the place of in-between, because in the quiet waiting rooms of life, we can sometimes hear his voice best.

The writer of Hebrews tells us that "faith is being sure of what we hope for and certain of what we do not see" (11:1). Faith helps us see with spiritual eyes what we can't see with physical eyes. It's faith that makes the ambiguity of the in-between more certain.

I have three thoughts for you regarding you and your closest relationships during the in-between.

First, if you're the one going through the in-between, you may think, *I don't have much faith, so it's hard for me to see that I'll ever be out of this place.* Jesus taught us that it's not the amount of your faith but the *object* of your faith that matters. He said, "I tell you the truth, if you have faith as small as a mustard seed, you can say to this mountain, 'Move from here to there' and it will move. Nothing will be impossible for you" (Matthew 17:20). Sometimes people look at us and say, "You must have a lot of faith to have stepped out and planted a church, believing God for great things." We always respond with the truth: "No, we don't have much faith at all, but we've taken the little bit of faith we have and placed it in a great big God!" I encourage you to take the little faith you have and give it to God, then rest in his peace and security.

Second, if someone you love is stuck in a time of in-between, *join them* in this time. Give them the freedom to talk about what they're feeling and learning. Many times we hesitate to connect with people who are in the middle of cancer treatments, a job transition, or a family crisis because we feel inadequate to fix their problems. Just remember that the waiting rooms of life can get awfully lonely, and having you there alongside them can give the comfort and courage they need to face whatever comes their way.

Third, it may be that you should share some of these insights with the people you're closest to. If someone you love is stuck in a place where they're confused, frustrated, and restless, simply understanding more about this phase of life can be a big help. You might even encourage them to read the New Testament book of Hebrews so they can be inspired by the stories of imperfect people who faced great obstacles with an even greater faith.

Remember that the in-between can be a good thing, a place where you can find what you're truly looking for. The only place you're going to find peace is in the middle of anxiety. The only place you're going to find real joy is in the middle of problems. And the only place you're going to find real patience is in the middle of waiting.

WHEN THE IN-BETWEEN IS NOT SO GOOD

As student drivers, our kids were taught in driver's ed class to say "PNR" as they approached a green traffic light. PNR was short for "point of no return." It meant they had reached the point where they were committed to going through the light even if it turned yellow. No hesitancy or indecision, no slamming on the brakes and creating a hazard for other drivers, no turning back. Just a calm, spoken affirmation that they had to maintain their current course and speed. We experienced plenty of exciting moments while riding with our kids when they were newly licensed drivers, so hearing "PNR" was always a welcome assurance that there wouldn't be any surprises—at least not on that block.

Sometimes we need to declare a PNR in our lives. Otherwise, when we get caught in the intersection of circumstances and life, we freeze. A mental PNR will help you to avoid the paralysis many people experience in the uncertain times of life. Instead of being unable to make decisions or move forward, you will have the quiet confidence of knowing that the decision to keep going has already been made.

One thing to keep in mind is that sometimes the time of in-between may actually be a period of depression or grieving. After divorce or the loss of a loved one, a person usually experiences a time of in-between. While it's important to grieve and to work through the intense emotions, remember that these experiences can also make us more vulnerable to depression. A friend may need your help more than they know. Being there for someone who's stuck in life requires discernment and sensitivity on your part. You need to be encouraging without being overbearing. Be considerate of the tender time they're enduring, and be alert for opportunities to share their burden.

The simple question is, Will you be there for the people you love when they find themselves in a time of in-between?

THE IN-BETWEEN RELATIONSHIP

Of course, it's not just individuals who get stuck in between; whole relationships get stuck as well. In the place of in-between, friendships can fall apart, couples can feel like giving up on their marriage, and family problems can explode with disastrous consequences.

When your relationship is in between, it means that both of you are stuck in a paralysis that neither of you seems able to escape.

Most relationships get paralyzed because someone is unwilling to take the next step God has told them to take. If you know you're in a stuck relationship, take the initiative. Listen closely to God's voice speaking to you; maybe he's telling you to be honest with a friend and explain why you went off the deep end. Perhaps he's whispering to you to ask your spouse to forgive you for an argument that took place last night...or even last year.

I believe that we often know what we ought to do. God makes these things pretty clear. But fear, pride, or shame keeps us from doing what it takes to restore the relationship. The good news is that God wants your relationship to be restored even more than you do, and he's the only one with the power and wisdom to fix the broken pieces of your heart.

Instead of wallowing in self-pity or fear, it's time to declare PNR. Make the decision to commit to moving forward. No turning back!

LASTING LOVE RELATIONSHIP
Challenge

1. Commit to meditating on 1 Corinthians 13:4–8 every day this week. Write the passage on a note card you can keep with you in your purse or wallet.

2. Do any of your key relationships feel like they are in between right now? In what way? Ask God to show you what you can do to move forward.

3. In your journal write down things you can do to be there for the people you care the most about. For example, ask them to meet you for coffee, go out with them on an adventure, or buy them a book that is special to them. Remember that just being with someone is powerful.

Raving Fan

Intentionally Giving Encouragement

Love is an irresistible desire to be irresistibly desired.

ROBERT FROST

There is no better exercise for strengthening the heart
than reaching down and lifting up another.

ANONYMOUS

ncourage literally means to "give courage" to someone else.
It doesn't take much effort on your part to make a lasting impact on another
life. A smile or nod of agreement to someone delivering a public speech can give
them the courage to communicate confidently. A few well-timed words of encouragement to a friend can make the difference between someone giving up on
their dream or deciding to persevere. Sometimes just your quiet presence is
enough. When a friend has endured a tragic loss, just being with them in their
pain can give them courage to go on.

While this may seem perfectly obvious, too often we fall into ruts in our relationships, and our walk alongside someone loses the ongoing banter of encouragement. Our relationships can become complicated by jealousies or hurts,

and even though we still hike side by side with someone through life, we hesitate to offer encouragement freely. Some of us—because of how we grew up, our family of origin, or experiences in previous relationships—simply have a hard time building up other people.

Regardless of how you've lived until this point, it's time to make a conscious decision to be an encourager. If you do, your life and the lives of the people you love will never be the same.

DREAM CATCHER

Relationships are deepened and enriched as two people become raving fans of each other. Every one of us needs someone to cheer us on through life.

The first step to becoming an encourager is to discover the dreams of those you're close to. Not your dreams for them, but what *they* want to do and be.

This is especially tough for parents because so many adults were never encouraged as kids. I think that's the main reason so many parents end up trying to live out their own broken dreams through their children. Who hasn't known a dad who coaches his five-year-old son's T-ball team as if he were playing in the World Series? I'm all for passion in sports, but problems are inevitable if it's the dad's dream rather than the kid's dream.

As parents, we need to deal with our own issues without saddling our kids with the responsibility of fulfilling our lost dreams. As husbands, we need to let go of our jealousies regarding our wife's success. As a brother or sister, we need to stop comparing our sibling's enviable life to our own.

The truth is that God has created each of us to be unique. If we allow the important people in our lives to live out their *own* dreams—if we are willing to stand on the sidelines and cheer them on toward the finish line—we will show them what real, selfless love looks like.

But this will never happen until you get serious about discovering your loved one's hopes and dreams. Think about your key relationships. Do you know what their dreams are?

Here's a great question to start with: what would you attempt if you knew you couldn't fail? When you have their answer, get creative with ways to encourage and enable them to make their dream a reality. Could you help them do something, get somewhere, or make a connection with someone? Hold their dream with respect. The way you handle their secret hopes will reveal how much you really care about them.

Intentionally coming alongside someone else and helping them realize their dreams is not only a step toward growth and depth in your key relationships; it's also a step toward satisfaction and fulfillment in your own life. The Bible promises that "he who refreshes others will himself be refreshed" (Proverbs 11:25).

ENCOURAGEMENT TO OVERCOME

Encouragement also requires you to understand someone else's fears. Larry Crabb and Dan Allender, in their book *Encouragement,* speak of fear as a "core emotion" that everyone wrestles with: "Each of us has undergone some sort of trauma that has aggravated our basic fear of rejection and failure. Stuttering in front of schoolmates, the divorce of one's parents, the death of a close friend, financial disaster, a teen-age daughter's pregnancy—the list goes on and on. Situations that feed fears are part of everyone's background."[6]

Encouragement of a friend or spouse or child is often about helping that person overcome their fears. Just as you root for Olympic athletics to overcome their fear of failure or injury, cheering them to triumph and to be their best, in relationships you need to give courage to others to overcome the fear that holds them back.

But if you're going to help someone overcome their fears, you have to know what those fears are. In your key relationships—friend, spouse, parent, or child—have you ever come out and asked the other person, "What is the one thing you're most afraid of?" Have you been observant enough to notice the things they shrink from and are paralyzed by? Sometimes it helps just to ask, "What's holding you back?"

Encouragement often requires words to be spoken that are aimed at fear. To the person afraid of public speaking: "You know, you handled yourself very well in front of the group." To the one who's struggling with confidence at work: "It seems you have all the skills you need—and then some." To the one who fears being alone: "I will be here for you."

Encouragement—giving courage to someone to overcome—ultimately becomes a bond between two people that is strong and tight. It is one person being vulnerable and allowing another to enter into their private world and that person respecting that inner sanctum and speaking into it, helping to challenge the fear that resides there.

WHEN ENCOURAGEMENT IS NOT WHAT IT SEEMS

Too easily, our encouragements can be colored by our self-interests.

I recently read about a study that reveals an interesting truth about encouragement. Shelly Gable, a psychologist at the University of California–Santa Barbara, studied hundreds of couples and found that how we react to someone else's good news reveals more about the health of the relationship than how we react to their bad news. For example, if you respond like a wet blanket to your spouse's promotion, your true feelings of resentment and fear are revealed. That's a better predictor of a breakup than if you had encouraged your spouse if the promotion had been denied.[7]

It's not that we shouldn't offer encouragement when someone is down-and-out. Words that give hope to the hurting are always needed, but they don't necessarily reveal your heart. Have you ever doubted someone's integrity when they told you they were sorry for your misfortune? Their words may have been appropriate, but you knew their heart wasn't in it.

The true test of our love is when we can honestly rejoice when someone else is honored, wins the prize, or achieves their dreams. If you really love someone, you don't focus on "Why didn't that happen to me?" or "Why are they blessed and I'm not?" Instead, you will be the one who plans the celebration party and throws the confetti.

If you're willing to risk knowing the truth about your relationships, be alert to your gut reaction when you first hear of someone else's good fortune, and be sensitive to others' responses when you have good news to share. Your love is sincere if you can truly rejoice when others are blessed, or as the Bible puts it, "rejoice with those who rejoice" (Romans 12:15).

Sometimes we actually withhold encouragement for what we think are good reasons. Perhaps we want to make sure our friend or loved one faces reality. "You got the job, but you're going to have to work a lot harder now," or, "You'll never get accepted to that college, so don't bother applying." You might feel you're doing them a favor by protecting them from disappointment.

There are certainly times when it's appropriate to offer caution, but realize that such words can be devastating to the other person. It's shockingly easy to take courage away. That's what *discourage* means: "to subtract from someone else's courage."

Life is hard. For most of us, our supply of courage is pretty low to begin with, so it doesn't take much to convince us that we're inadequate for the task at hand. Pointing out shortcomings, regurgitating past mistakes, and highlighting the negatives of a situation will quickly eat away at your loved one's courage.

Is this something you're doing, even unintentionally, in your key relationships?

LASTING LOVE RELATIONSHIP
Challenge

1. Do you know the dreams and ambitions of the people in your
   key relationships? If not, be intentional in discovering what they
   are. If you already know their ambitions, how can you cheer
   them on and help them realize those dreams?
2. It's okay to have unrealized dreams. We all have them. But are
   you trying to live out unrealized dreams through your children?
   How can you let them know they're released to pursue the plan
   God has for them?
3. Do you know the hidden fears of your key relationships? If not,
   ask them and record their answers in your journal. Make notes
   of ways you might come alongside to help those people overcome what holds them back.

THE ART OF RISKING AWKWARDNESS

Clumsy Grace

Practicing the Art of Risking Awkwardness

> Be willing to be uncomfortable. Be comfortable being
> uncomfortable. It may get tough, but it's a small price
> to pay for living a dream.
>
> PETER MCWILLIAMS

> Inspiration usually comes during work, rather than
> before it.
>
> MADELEINE L'ENGLE

Several years ago I noticed that my relationship with my sons Ryan and Josh was settling into a "just okay" stage. I would come home from work and say, "How was your day, guys?" They'd reply, "Okay. How was your day?" I'd respond, "Okay." End of conversation.

Everything about our relationship seemed normal and comfortable. But our conversation never seemed to get past the surface level. I sensed we all longed for a deeper connection, but it just felt awkward to go there—maybe for my boys, but certainly for me.

One day I took a risk. I felt awkward doing so, but I said to my sons, "I know you guys must have a lot of stress at school. I can't even imagine what it's like being a teenager today with all the pressures you face. I really want us to have a relationship where you feel free to share your struggles and stresses with me."

They immediately replied, "Well, you never share any of your struggles with us. Why should we share our struggles with you?"

Whoa! Their response floored me. It also opened my eyes. I explained to them that the reason I didn't share my problems with them was because I didn't want to dump more stress on them than they already had.

They readily said, "Well, we can handle it."

They went on to tell me that when we, as parents, act like we never have any problems, it makes them feel like they can't share their failures and struggles with us because we wouldn't be able to relate.

I risked feeling awkward in the relationship, and something good came out of it—a deeper connection. We got past "just okay." Out of that one conversation, our relationship changed significantly. It took us to a whole new level as we finally began sharing our struggles, failures, and stresses.

To be honest, it's still difficult sometimes. I find that my relationships with my children continue to go through awkward phases where I need to risk more. My teenagers have never come to me and said, "I really want to have a deeper relationship with you, and I would love to sit down often and talk about what you're going through." If they did, it would be cause for an emergency room visit! I've come to realize that if I'm going to have a closer relationship with my kids, then it's up to me to step out of my comfort zone and get into their lives. The more I get over my feelings of awkwardness and risk deeper conversations, the closer I get to the people in my life.

DANGER ZONE

Love at first sight says that when relationships start feeling awkward, it's time to bail. Lasting love says that when there's a problem, a silence, a rote routine, or something not quite right in a relationship, that's precisely the time to dig in and do the hard work of risking awkward questions or uncomfortable conversations. Every relationship breakthrough in my life has involved the art of risking awkwardness, which simply means stepping out of my comfort zone so that a relationship can go to the next level. In a way God did this for us so we could have a fulfilling relationship with him. John 1:14 says, "The Word became flesh and made his dwelling among us." The supernatural Son of God stepped out of the comfort of his perfect home in heaven to enter our imperfect and broken world. Because he loved us, he took the risk to enter our world. He even put on a suit of human frailty and complete vulnerability so we could relate to him and he could build a bridge to us.

It's natural to settle into a comfort zone. After all, one of the main reasons we develop a relationship with someone is because we feel comfortable in their presence. If we're not careful, however, the comfort zone can become a danger zone in our closest relationships. I've discovered that the greatest growth in relationships happens when I'm willing to be in an uncomfortable place for a while. Whether it's moving a good relationship to a great one or experiencing a breakthrough in a troubled relationship, you have to be willing to be uncomfortable for a while.

It's certainly not healthy for a relationship to perpetually stay in an awkward state. After all, one of the great blessings of loving relationships is the feeling of complete comfort in someone else's presence. But if you're always in a state of predictable comfort, there can never be growth. If you become too complacent, the comfort zone may eventually turn into a death zone. If the relationship is allowed to drift too far over time, it will ultimately fall apart.

STRANGER IN A STRANGE LAND

The question is, How can you tell when a comfort zone has become a danger zone in your relationship? One sure sign is when you start to feel like a stranger in the relationship.

Even relationships that were at one time deep and personal can take backward steps and cycle back to earlier stages. Often this happens with best friends. It can easily happen with adult siblings as they leave their childhood home, become adults, and live apart. What was once a close relationship between brothers can become distant. And this certainly happens (all too easily) in marriage as a husband and wife get so busy in their lives that they drift apart, sometimes without even knowing it.

In all of these cases, we can feel like a stranger in a strange land. Yet it's a land we once thought was our home. Does this ring true in any of your key relationships?

The book *The Fine Art of Small Talk: How to Start a Conversation, Keep It Going, Build Networking Skills—and Leave a Positive Impression,* by Debra Fine, addresses the fears so many of us have of talking with others in social situations. The author makes the point that most of the time the other person is just as afraid of feeling awkward as we are. She writes, "If you generally wait for someone else to take the initiative in a conversation, you have been self-centered. It's true! You have allowed your own comfort to take precedence over every other person's. You haven't been doing your fair share of the work."[8]

I think this applies just as much to our key relationships as to strangers at a party or a business conference. We sometimes feel like strangers, even in close relationships. But while we may feel awkward, we need to understand that the other person may well feel awkward too. And most of all, we need to take responsibility in furthering and deepening the relationship by sacrificing our own comfort, overcoming our fears, and risking awkwardness.

FINDING THE GRACE TO BE AWKWARD

Last week the art of acting intentionally was all about creating the will and intention to work on your relationships. This week we focus on action: stepping out of your comfort zone, regardless of your feelings, and actually doing things in your key relationships.

Most people mistakenly believe that love is a feeling. Lasting love is an *action*. In fact, it doesn't really matter if you have loving feelings toward someone if you don't put them into action. Love isn't love until you express it, so sometimes it's important to acknowledge that expressing love feels uncomfortable and awkward.

Recently a friend of mine heard Michael Reagan give a speech about his relationship with his father, President Ronald Reagan. Michael spoke with admiration in his voice about what a wonderfully warm and encouraging father the president had been to him.

He said that though his dad always made him feel incredibly loved, he couldn't remember his dad ever hugging him. That expression of affection just didn't come naturally to him. As an adult Michael decided that he would take the risk of initiating a hug with the man he so loved and admired. Michael said the next time he went to his dad's house, he walked over and embraced him. The president seemed a little startled at first but awkwardly put his arms around his son and gave him a quick hug.

Michael said from that day on, every time he would visit, he would always give his dad a big hug. In fact, when Michael would start walking toward his father, the president would open his arms wide, eager for the hug from his son.

At his father's eulogy, Michael spoke these touching words:

At the early onset of Alzheimer's disease, my father and I would tell each other we loved each other, and we would give each other a hug. As the years went by and he could no longer verbalize my name, he recognized me as the man who hugged him. So when I would walk into the house, he would be there in his chair opening up his arms for that hug hello and the hug goodbye. It was a blessing truly brought on by God.[9]

Our situations are different, of course, but in many ways we all sometimes find it difficult to verbalize our feelings or to physically express our love. Stepping out of our comfort zones and risking awkwardness to express love may be the hardest thing we ever do. It also may very well be the most beautiful and rewarding thing we ever do.

The good news is that you can count on God to give you the grace to step out and risk being awkward. God's amazing grace is what gives us the power to change and move out of those stagnant places that make relationships stale.

The Bible says, "God is working in you, giving you the desire to obey him and the power to do what pleases him" (Philippians 2:13, NLT). God not only gives you the desire to risk loving; he will also give you the power to love.

Remember, upside-down thinking says that if two people really love each other, then all the relationship stuff will flow naturally, and people will instinctively know how to meet each other's needs. And if something feels awkward, then it's time to leave.

Nothing could be further from the truth. Even the best relationships have rough edges, difficult moments, and embarrassing confessions. It takes a commitment to risk, a willingness to be uncomfortable at times, and real action if you want to see a transformation in your key relationships.

This is the art of risking awkwardness.

LASTING LOVE RELATIONSHIP
Challenge

1. Are any of your key relationships stuck in the "just okay" mode? What risk could you take that might cause a breakthrough? Are you willing to do that?

2. Do you have difficulty expressing your feelings? If you do, ask God to give you his grace to risk being awkward this week.

3. What are some things you wish the people in your key relationships would ask *you*? What things deep down inside you do you long for people to know?

4. Check back on the vision statement and action plan that you wrote on Day 10 and Day 11. How are you doing? Really commit to risk acting out of love this week.

Mind Reader

The Awkwardness of Asking

I want to know how God created this world. I am not
interested in this or that phenomenon, in the spectrum
of this or that element. I want to know His thoughts;
the rest are details.

ALBERT EINSTEIN

The only true wisdom is in knowing you know
nothing.

SOCRATES

I've always been a big fan of the classic and admittedly cheesy *Star Trek* television series. I think I've seen almost all the old episodes as Capt. James T. Kirk
led the crew of the starship *Enterprise* where "no man has gone before." From
Klingons to "phasers set to stun," I know way too much *Star Trek* trivia.

One of my favorite *Star Trek* moments was when First Officer Spock would
perform the Vulcan mind meld. Spock would place his hand on the temple and
forehead of the unsuspecting person and immediately be overwhelmed by all
their thoughts, emotions, and experiences. He then would know what they had
been thinking and everything about their past without their saying a word.

If only we could use the Vulcan mind meld, then we could go where no one has gone before—in relationships. Wouldn't it be great if we could know what the people we love were thinking? Unfortunately, none of us has been so gifted in real life as the fictional Spock, but we often act as if we were. One of the little things that causes big trouble in relationships is assuming way too much. We think we know what the other person is thinking and what they need without asking.

ASSUMING TOO MUCH

We often make the mistake of assuming we know how the people closest to us feel rather than taking the time to find out. The most common pitfall is the assumption that the other person's needs are the same as ours.

In marriage we may mistakenly think that our spouse's needs are the same as our own, and in so doing, we completely skip over the crucial questions that take relationships to the deepest level. Many parents wrongly assume that their children are wired just the way they are when it comes to expressing and receiving love and encouragement. Best friends often stop asking questions of each other and instead anticipate what they believe the other would say.

It's easy to assume that the person I'm relating to is exactly like me, but it's never true. In fact, it's a dangerous assumption with devastating consequences. There are many husbands and wives who truly love each other, yet neither feels loved because each completely misses the target when it comes to meeting the other's needs. There are many parents who really love their teenager, but he or she doesn't feel loved because the parents aren't expressing it in a way their child can receive it. Many friendships become distant when well-meaning people make false assumptions and stop making the effort to learn more about each other. In every case the root problem is that in relationships we all tend to give what we wish we could get. In doing so, we overlook that the other person's needs may be entirely different from our own. If you want the people you love to really feel loved, it's essential to risk the awkwardness of asking them what their needs are.

It's interesting that in the Gospels, Jesus Christ would ask people what they needed before he healed them. One time he came upon a blind beggar named Bartimaeus, who was sitting on the side of the road, and Jesus asked him, "What do you want me to do for you?" (Luke 18:41, NLT).

Of course, Jesus already knew the answer; he knows everything about everyone. But he gave Bartimaeus the opportunity to identify and verbalize his greatest need. If the God of the universe asks people what their needs are, don't you think we ought to do the same?

When was the last time you sat down with your spouse and asked, "How can I better meet your needs? I really care about you, and I want you to feel that love. How can I make you feel loved?"

Some friends of ours told us how they experienced a lot of frustration early in their marriage because they had never learned to do this. The wife felt loved when she received a loving gift. It didn't have to be an expensive gift. She just liked to think about her husband caring enough to take the time to find the perfect gift for her. When it came to receiving gifts, the husband could take it or leave it. He said, "I like it when she tells me how much she loves me and how proud she is of me. They say talk is cheap, and I'm a low-budget kind of guy. I don't want gifts. I just want her to verbalize her love."

So there were two different needs. Yet each assumed the other's need was just like their own. Before Christmas, the wife would spend weeks and sometimes months picking out the perfect gift for her husband. Sometimes that meant endless hours of research or traveling for miles. When she would give him the gift, he would open it and say a little too dismissively, "Thanks, honey. That's great." Of course, she'd feel tremendous disappointment, thinking, *Doesn't he understand how much love I put into that?*

He would then give her a gift that he bought the day before, and no matter how expensive it was, she knew he had put no time into the decision. He would then spend a great deal of time telling her how much he loved her and how wonderful she was, but still she felt devalued.

It took them quite a while, but eventually they risked the awkwardness of asking. They honestly shared how they felt about gift giving. He told her that gifts were fine by him, but he honestly didn't get that excited about them and would rather she express her love verbally. She told him gifts were important to her because they made her feel as if he was really thinking about her and putting in time and effort to find just the right thing for her.

As a result of risking the awkwardness of asking, they both started to change. They began to meet the other's real need rather than assuming it was a duplicate of their own.

We readily embrace the idea of our uniqueness in the world—"There's no one in the world just like me." And yet we so often make the mistake of assuming that others think and feel and love just like us. They're unique too. That's why it's crazy not to ask.

LOST SKILLS

I think one of the relational skills we've lost in contemporary life is that of being interested in another person. I don't mean in the romantic way of having a love interest but in the more general sense of being truly inquisitive. Some people speak of this as being *curious,* as in "he's just not that curious about people." Which means he doesn't seem to reach out to others to understand them, learn about them, and inquire about what is important to them. He's just wrapped up in himself.

I'm sure you've seen reruns of the old television show *The Newlywed Game.* Husbands and wives answered questions separately, trying to match the answer their spouse would give to the same question. It was hilarious to see how far apart couples really were. Okay, we'll give them a break. They were newlyweds, after all. But how true is it that after months of courtship and years of marriage, we often know so little about each other?

Many of us are just not that curious in our relationships. We don't extend our interest *outside of ourselves.* Not only is this a lost skill, but it also creates significant problems in many of our relationships. Inquiring about another person's interests and needs, hurts and aches, feelings and thoughts may feel unnatural to us. It's also a little risky. But overcoming the awkwardness of asking is absolutely essential if you're going to create rich, full relationships.

Another skill we seem to have lost is simply the act of listening. Once you express curiosity and ask a question, it's equally important to really listen to the answer.

I confess, sometimes I'll ask my spouse that all-important question "How can I best meet your needs?" but I find my attention drifting before the conversation is completed. When I walk away, I mistakenly assume I understand. I'm now learning to let the people in my life have conversation closure. I think sometimes we don't understand the vital role that listening plays in making our loved ones feel understood. Just imagine what it would be like if you were getting ready to eat your favorite meal only to have it snatched away at the last minute. That's how most people feel when someone stops really listening halfway through a conversation. Just remember, you don't have to solve all the issues that are brought up; the goal is simply to connect through listening.

The willingness to initiate awkward conversations has become nearly extinct in this age of efficiency. Technology can often serve as a cocoon, insulating our emotions and problems from others. After all, no one can see your tears or hear the hurt in your voice in an e-mail. Because everyone is busy, it seems like we all have an excuse when we didn't anticipate the breakup of a friend's marriage or didn't realize that a loved one was struggling with depression.

When I hear about an avoidable tragedy in a close friend's life, I usually feel a sharp pang of guilt. *Come to think of it, something didn't seem quite right the last few times we talked, but I felt like I'd be butting in to bring it up. If they had wanted to tell me something, they would have.* The reality is that sometimes a situation is so overwhelming and painful that a person doesn't even know how to begin to open up. In fact, it can be almost impossible for them if they've tried to keep up a facade for a long time, if the issue feels embarrassing or shameful to them, or if they're scared about how you or someone else might react if they break their secrecy.

A friend of ours was in an abusive relationship for years, suffering silently because no one wanted to risk asking if she was having marital problems. Finally her sister cared enough to ask the tough questions, and our friend said that a very awkward conversation followed. This precious friend now looks back at that day as the beginning of her healing and restoration, but it might never have happened if someone hadn't loved her enough to risk rejection.

UNDOING ASSUMPTIONS

Maybe you feel awkward about asking a close friend about important things. It could be that you lack the basic impetus to be curious about other people. It might be that you *do* ask but you *don't* listen. An added problem may be that you assume you already know what they're thinking and feeling.

Let me challenge you to throw out every preconceived assumption about your key relationships. Instead, assume something else: maybe *you just don't know.* Assume you really have no idea what their fears, needs, or joys are. Assume you don't know the thing they've always wanted to do but never have. Assume you don't know what game they most like to play or what country they'd love to travel to or what their favorite food is. Assume you don't know the last book they read, the television show they rush home to see each week, or their most memorable Thanksgiving. Assume you don't know how their family is doing or how their classes at school are going. Assume you don't know how God has been speaking to them this week…

Come to think of it, those are some pretty good questions. Risk the awkwardness and ask.

LASTING LOVE RELATIONSHIP
Challenge

1. What are some things that you feel people in your life assume wrongly about you? How does it make you feel?

2. This week as you spend time with the people who matter most to you, focus on asking them creative questions and then really listening to their answers.

3. Has something been gnawing at you regarding someone you really care about? Do you have a concern that goes beyond surface chat and casual conversation? Dare to risk the awkwardness of asking deeper questions.

Vulnerable

The Awkwardness of Revealing Your Heart

> It is impossible to talk or to write without apparently
> throwing oneself helplessly open.
> HERMAN MELVILLE

> What is uttered from the heart alone, will win the
> hearts of others to your own.
> JOHANN WOLFGANG VON GOETHE

There's something profound about watching young children at play, observing their innocence. You don't ever have to wonder if a small child is happy, sad, content, or frustrated. Each and every child will absolutely, in no uncertain terms, let you know exactly how they feel. You don't ever have to tell a young child to live out of their heart.

In the Bible, Jesus said that we should come to him like little children: open, sincere, and vulnerable. I have to think that if Jesus wants us to come to him this way, then it must be the way we are supposed to be in all our relationships: real, transparent, and vulnerable. But most of us aren't, because something has happened between the time we were little children and now.

Life happens. Hurt happens. Disappointment happens. Rejection happens. And through it all, we build walls around our hearts.

In order to develop deep, rich, and loving relationships, we have to tear down those walls so we can offer our hearts completely. It takes 100 percent of our energy, creativity, effort, and emotions to build the kind of relationships God wants us to have.

How much of your heart are you giving to your relationships today?

If you're like me, some days are better than others. There are moments when I'm fully living out of my heart, and in those moments, in those glimpses of deep honesty, sincerity, and vulnerability, I'm filled with complete joy. In those moments when the walls come down and my heart is totally exposed, I feel fully alive. In those moments when I live from my heart, I feel that I am fully God's and that I am being who he created me to be. I want to live in those moments more and more, don't you?

LIVING UNDER COVER

It's awkward to expose your heart and feel completely vulnerable. In fact, you may even feel awkward just reading about it. That's because the upside-down thinking of the world says you have to protect your heart. It says that if you expose your heart and share your true feelings, people may not like you. If they see the real you, with all your faults, fears, and failures, they may reject you. And if people reject you, then you're not valuable, and you don't count.

If we want to move past shallow, superficial relationships into the deep, connected, rich relationships God wants for us, we have to let go of the opinions of others and be willing to expose our true selves.

God wants to give us a new heart (see Ezekiel 36:26). He wants to take our broken, stony, stubborn heart and give us a tender, responsive heart. That's the kind of heart we need to build great relationships.

But we often use all kinds of band-aids to cover our broken hearts, and just like little children, we are very proud of them. Instead of Flintstones and Barney Band-Aids, sometimes we use achievement band-aids. We use symbols of success to bandage and cover our broken hearts. When people look at those symbols, they're impressed by what they see on the surface, and they usually don't bother to look deeper into our wounded hearts.

We have some nice band-aids of possessions too. We drive our band-aids, we wear our band-aids, and we live in our band-aid homes, hoping they will cover up the emptiness we have inside. We also use the band-aid of pretending. We put on a band-aid smile and pretend that everything's perfect so people will envy us and say, "Wow, they've got it made!" We act like everything is great, while on the inside we are wounded and bleeding. But we don't want anyone to see our pain because we don't want to face being rejected.

In his book *Wild at Heart,* John Eldredge tells about a conversation with his best friend—an articulate, educated man with a great family and an enviable job. His friend, who seemed to have it all together, admitted, "The truth is, John, I feel like I'm just [bluffing] my way through life…and that someday soon I'll be exposed as an imposter."[10] Eldredge goes on to say that this is a common theme among men. Men, especially, seem afraid to open up their hearts because they fear rejection. Women, of course, fear rejection too, but perhaps instead of covering their hearts with success and achievements, they use the band-aids of Gucci and Botox.

There's nothing wrong with any of these things. But they are *things.* They aren't ultimately important. We have to ask ourselves, Why are we acquiring so much? Do we really think by having all the right stuff we'll get others' approval? Do we honestly believe people will think less of us if we don't fill our lives with possessions? Might we really be hiding our true hearts?

Another way people hide their hearts is with the band-aid of food (yes, we're going there). *Uh-oh, I'm about to feel something real. Quick, get me a Big Mac!* Or, *Those people just said something that hurt me, but this chocolate cake will make it feel better. Yes, let me cover this hurt with a chocolate cake band-aid and some ice cream, and everything will be all right.*

Sometimes we even try to use God as a band-aid. We really want him to heal us, but we don't actually want to take him to the broken places because it's too painful. There's too much shame. We don't want him to touch the hurt because, well, it hurts and hurts badly. We're embarrassed, and if someone else knows, it will add humiliation to our pain. We end up hoping that if we do all the right things, we can cover up that hurt with God. So we put on our best Sunday clothes and our best Sunday face, and we hide our hearts behind talking about God instead of truly submitting our hearts to him. We quote scriptures and say the right things, but deep down inside we're only saying them because we want people to be impressed with how spiritual we are.

EXPOSING YOUR HEART

Where are you hiding your heart today? What are you using to cover up your hurts? What are you using to keep people from seeing your true self? And how do you remove the band-aids and expose your heart so you can embrace authentic relationships?

You have to make a choice. You have to be willing to risk the awkwardness of being vulnerable. You have to decide that being real, open, and honest is more important than the opinions of others—who, by the way, are just as concerned about your opinion of them.

It's painful to tear off a Band-Aid, isn't it? I've tried removing them slowly, one hair at a time. I've tried pulling them off under water. I've tried all kinds of ways, but what works best is the grip-it-and-rip-it method. Oh, it's painful all right, but the pain doesn't last that long. Better just to get it done.

Likewise, it's painful when you start tearing away band-aids that have been over your heart for years. I'm not suggesting this is easy, but understand that revealing is healing. Revealing your heart is the first step to living from your heart. Only when you live from your heart can you truly be free.

THE REWARD OF SHARING YOUR HEART

There's no doubt that some of us have real difficulty with revealing our heart and telling the people closest to us how much they mean to us.

My grandfather grew up in a home where they never verbally expressed love. He never heard the words "I love you" from his parents. As a result, he himself never learned how to express words of affirmation and love.

I remember many visits to my grandparents' house over the holidays. My mom so desperately wanted to hear her father say those words that she would literally prompt him. As we were walking out the door at the end of our visit, she would say, "Daddy, we're leaving now, but, Daddy, I love you. I love you, Daddy."

It was almost painful to watch as he would say, oh so awkwardly, "I do you too, girl." Those words were so forced and uncomfortable for him, it was all he could do to get them out. My mom knew what he meant, but still she longed to hear those words and to hear them flow from his mouth more spontaneously, more freely. At the end of my grandfather's life, he was finally able to say those three words to my mom: "I love you." And it meant the world to her.

Maybe you see yourself in the person of my grandfather. Possibly not to that extreme, but maybe you're not naturally affectionate and it's difficult for you to show your feelings. The fact that people are stoic on the surface doesn't mean they lack emotion underneath. In fact, it's often the case (and perhaps even true for you) that people who have difficulty expressing emotions long to share their heart. It's hard for them to volunteer that, but when someone cares enough to genuinely ask, they may find the strength to open up their heart. It's often the *right question,* sometimes about a subject you would never associate with that person directly, that prompts a response that opens up a dimension of their personality and character you never knew about.

Start by asking yourself what you wish someone would ask you. What's inside you that you want to tell certain people but have a hard time saying aloud in conversation? Can you turn the tables and imagine that one of the people you love may be wishing that you would ask them some of the same questions?

A friend of mine is a CEO, and I've noticed over time how much his employees respect him and follow his leadership. I asked him one day what his secret is. He said, "My team doesn't always understand or even agree with the decisions I make, but they always know my heart. They know I care deeply about them and about our company. They know my heart because I share my heart."

When you reveal your heart, you create an atmosphere of security and trust for the people around you. You are in essence saying, "It's okay to be your true self around me, because I'm willing to be my true self with you." When you are authentic, it draws people to you. Not only do you feel at rest, but you help others feel relaxed and secure too.

But I have to warn you: when you expose your heart, there will be times when it gets broken. Sometimes you will risk love, and you won't get love back. Sometimes you will risk commitment, and the other person won't commit to you. Sometimes you'll make yourself vulnerable, and you'll get rejected. Every person has experienced heartache, but the rewards are far greater when you risk your heart. C. S. Lewis put it this way: "To love at all is to be vulnerable."

If you love anything or anyone, you are risking heartache. If you want to have the kind of rich, meaningful relationships that God intends, you have to risk exposing your heart and allowing yourself to be vulnerable.

LASTING LOVE RELATIONSHIP
Challenge

1. We all use band-aids to protect our hearts. What is your band-aid of choice when it comes to covering your real self? The band-aid of material things: clothes, cars, etc.? The band-aid of success? The band-aid of intellect? The band-aid of outward spirituality?

2. Consider your key relationships. Do you need to share your heart with and really open up to any of them? This week risk the awkwardness of revealing your heart to them.

3. Log on to onemonthtolove.com to learn more about removing the band-aids in relationships.

Act as If

The Awkwardness of Putting Actions Before Feelings

> We all do no end of feeling, and we mistake it for
> thinking.
>
> MARK TWAIN

> We are obliged to love one another. We are not strictly
> bound to "like" one another.
>
> THOMAS MERTON

Most people who meet me think I'm completely confident when I speak to large groups or mingle in a crowd of strangers. The truth is that I feel horribly inadequate and insecure most of the time. As a child, I was the kid who hung back and tried hard to blend in so I wouldn't be singled out or called on in class. Somehow I always felt like I had shown up at a party I wasn't invited to. My dad was transferred when I was in junior high, and we moved across the country to Texas. That's when I realized I had the opportunity to reinvent myself. Sure, *I* knew I was shy and insecure, but *they* didn't. Out of a deep desire to join the party, I decided that I would act as if I were the person I wanted to be.

From day one I acted over-the-top friendly to every new person I met. When I say "acted," I mean this performance could have won an Oscar. I felt far more shy and awkward than I ever had before, and several times a day I had to remind myself to act as if I really liked these folks. When I felt like hiding in the bathroom during school lunches, I'd make myself go to a lunch table and introduce myself. When I felt like pretending I hadn't seen the girl who dropped her books, I made myself go over and help her. When I felt like melting into anonymity in the back of the classroom, I forced myself to grab a front seat, where I'd be required to participate.

Unfortunately, I didn't have any altruistic motivation. I wasn't doing my little experiment to benefit anyone but myself. I just desperately wanted to know what it was like to be included, even if it was, from my perspective, fake.

The big surprise, however, was that I gradually became the kind of person I was choosing to act like. I would smile and help the kid whose locker was stuck and then realize I hadn't talked myself into doing it. I'd raise my hand to answer a question in class without thinking twice. And the laughter I shared at lunch wasn't forced. I actually loved being with those kids.

My actions became second nature, and feelings developed as a result. It was only by *acting* loving that I *became* loving.

LOVE TRAIN

Do you remember that seventies R&B hit song by the O'Jays called "Love Train"? The lyrics encouraged people to start a love train. Well, it makes for a catchy song, but it's tricky when you actually try to put it into practice.

Logic seems to dictate that feelings are the engine of the love train, and wherever your feelings go, your actions should trail right along like a caboose. If you feel scared, you should worry; if you feel angry, you should let off some steam; if you're overworked or tired, you're excused for being grumpy and short-tempered. Sound familiar? That's how most of us live our lives.

Lasting love says that our feelings were never meant to be the engine of our lives. The engine of the real love train is action. That's because actions are infi-

nitely more powerful than feelings. You can think kind thoughts about someone all day long, but until you put some action to your feelings, your relationship won't improve. If I feel sorry for someone who's hurting but do nothing to
lighten their load, my empathy won't help them or strengthen our relationship.

For most of us, what seems natural is to feel our way into an action. And
culture reinforces this idea that until we feel inclined to do something, we
shouldn't go to the trouble of actually acting on it. God's model for relationships
is the opposite: to act our way into a feeling. In other words, to act as we know
we ought to, regardless of whether we feel like it or not.

Jesus Christ is our great example of acting in love. The night before his
death he poured out his feelings to his Father in the Garden of Gethsemane. He
prayed, "My Father, if it is possible, may this cup be taken from me. Yet not as
I will, but as you will" (Matthew 26:39). Jesus was saying that he was willing to
go to the cross, not because he felt like dying an excruciatingly painful death,
but because it was the only way to bridge a relationship between God and us.
He acted, not out of feelings, but purely out of love for you and me.

I'm not saying feelings are bad. God gave us emotions because they're in-
trinsic to enjoying relationships. But often the mark of true maturity and obedience is moving forward despite our feelings. After all, how many people would
go to work each day if the decision to show up rested only on their feelings?
Whenever I act in love, whether I feel like it or not, an amazing thing happens.
Loving feelings begin to develop, because feelings follow actions, not the other
way around.

I talk to so many couples who say, "We just don't have any feelings for each
other." The big mistake they make is waiting for the loving feelings to come back
before they start acting in loving ways. If you always wait to feel loving before you
do anything loving, then you won't be a very loving person. You'll be inconsistent
in loving the people closest to you, because your feelings constantly fluctuate.

One of the most profound truths you can ever discover about relationships
is that feelings follow actions. When I act in love toward someone in my life, it

creates powerful feelings of love. If your marriage has started to lose those loving feelings, don't wait for the feelings to return. Start doing loving things regardless of your feelings. It's not being hypocritical; it's simply acting in faith.
As you start acting in faith, the loving feelings start to come back.

Lasting love is not an emotion, though it creates powerful emotions. Lasting love is a choice that goes beyond fluctuating feelings. Lasting love is all about
acting as if in order to experience all that love can be.

GRIDLOCK

Occasionally I'm stuck in a relationship and truly don't know what to do. But
if I'm honest, I have to admit that far more often I know what I ought to do
and *just don't want to do it.*

Putting actions before feelings can be awkward on many levels. Getting
honest with someone about a touchy subject or stepping out in a new relationship feels risky. What if I'm ridiculed, rejected, or misjudged? Disciplining my
kids and sharing wisdom I've learned the hard way can make me feel hypocritical. Who am I to teach them when I can't get my own act together? Offering
forgiveness to someone who has hurt me feels counterintuitive. Why shouldn't
they suffer for the pain they've caused? Given five minutes, I can come up with
a hundred reasons why I shouldn't put myself in an awkward situation and why
I don't feel like acting responsibly in a relationship.

Maybe your teenager has asked for permission to do something "everyone
else" is doing, and you know that if you don't let her go, there will be wailing
and gnashing of teeth…maybe even calls from other parents. You just don't feel
like dealing with that right now; plus you would rather not be labeled as the
geeky parent. You honestly don't think it's a good idea for her to go and can list
several reasons why, but still you wonder if it's worth the time and the tears that
will be involved in saying no. Will you love her enough to act in a way that's best
for her rather than easiest for you?

Or maybe an emotionally charged issue that's been simmering between you and your spouse has finally blown up. You feel that you're right and your spouse is wrong, and you've already talked till you're blue in the face. Will you walk out, or will you work it out? Will you commit to staying up all night to work it out or agree to go to marriage counseling because you value your relationship even when the feelings aren't there?

Even when the other person has caused the problem in a relationship, we still have a choice to act on our feelings or our commitments. God gives us daily opportunities to have winning relationships, but *we* have to take action instead of waiting to react according to our feelings. The Bible tells us, "Most of all, love each other as if your life depended on it. Love makes up for practically anything" (1 Peter 4:8, MSG). When we act as if we feel loving, we're acting in faith.

Our feelings and our flesh are all tangled up in these bodies of ours. No wonder it feels so unnatural to put our emotions off to the side and choose to act in a way that is contrary to what we feel like doing. But God can help us do this. When I'm stepping out in awkward obedience, my conversation with God goes something like this: *Father, I'm choosing to obey you and do the loving thing here, not because I feel like it, mind you, but because I trust you. I feel like a victim, but I'm not going to act like it, because I believe you always fight for me when my motive is love. I'm not perfect like you, Lord, so I won't do everything just right, and it may get messy. I feel horribly insecure, but I choose to do more than nothing and to risk awkwardness because I want to learn to love like you.*

Acting as if is as much about walking with God as it is dealing with a relationship. I have a favorite quote by Kent M. Keith, called "The Paradoxical Commandments," that says, "People are illogical, unreasonable, and self-centered. Love them anyway. If you do good, people will accuse you of selfish ulterior motives. Do good anyway. If you are successful, you will win false friends and true enemies. Succeed anyway. The good you do today will be forgotten tomorrow. Do good anyway. Honesty and frankness make you vulnerable. Be honest and frank anyway. The biggest men and women with the biggest ideas can be shot down by the smallest men and women with the smallest minds. Think big anyway. People favor underdogs but follow only top dogs. Fight for a few underdogs anyway. What you spend years building may be destroyed overnight. Build anyway. People really need help but may attack you if you do help them. Help people anyway. Give the world the best you have and you'll get kicked in the teeth. Give the world the best you have anyway."

The engine always guides the caboose. When we *act as if* instead of pursuing self-comfort, we become more like our Savior in the process.

LASTING LOVE RELATIONSHIP
Challenge

1. In your key relationships, do you tend to be driven by your feelings or your actions? Does your response vary depending on the relationship?

2. When you feel like a relationship is stuck, what usually prevents you from embracing awkwardness and taking the first step?

3. It has been said, "It is the unseen and the spiritual in people that determines the outward and the actual." In what way does this statement shed light on your key relationships?

Making Waves

The Awkwardness of Expressing Anger

You can safely assume that you've created God in your
own image when it turns out that God hates all the
same people you do.

ANNE LAMOTT

Conflict is inevitable, but combat is optional.

MAX LUCADO

A while back I had the opportunity to scuba-dive in a five-hundred-
thousand-gallon water tank at a place called the Aquarium. The tank was
filled with more than two hundred species of fish from around the globe.

Afterward I had an interesting conversation with one of the marine biolo-
gists. I observed, "Many people have fish tanks in their homes, and they go out
and get excited about buying a fifteen-dollar tropical fish. They bring it home,
put it in their tank, and then it dies the next day—and they're so frustrated. That
same thing must happen to you guys, just at a whole different level. You probably pay hundreds of dollars for a fish, but do you ever put it in the tank and
then it dies the next day?"

He replied, "Fish die in our tank all the time. But the difference is that when a fish dies in your tank at home, you know it's dead because it floats to the top. In our tank the way we know a fish has died is that someone says, 'You know what? I haven't seen that fish in a couple of weeks.'"

In other words, dead fish just get eaten!

There's a lot of intense aggression in the ocean, and there's a lot of intense emotion in the relational ocean. If you want to experience lasting love, your relationships will have to go through conflict, and you'll have to risk the awkwardness of expressing anger.

GOD-GIVEN ANGER

Dealing with anger can feel awkward because we generally think of anger as a destructive emotion that's always bad for relationships. Really, nothing could be further from the truth.

Did you know that anger is a God-given emotion? The Bible tells us that it's possible to be angry and it not be wrong or sinful (see Ephesians 4:26). It all depends on how you process and express it. Did you know that Jesus himself got angry? When he threw the money-changers out of the temple, the Scriptures tell us he had a righteous indignation, which simply means he was mad. So even the perfect Son of God expressed anger.

In fact, anger is not only normal; it's absolutely necessary in order for a relationship to go to a deeper level. In some instances anger is the most loving emotion you can express; it shows that you care enough about the relationship to confront an issue that's causing problems.

Anger is only destructive when you process it incorrectly. Expressed wrongly, it can be devastating to a relationship. I recently heard the horrifying statistic that nearly one in four women will experience some type of physical abuse during their lifetime. If you are in a physically abusive relationship, you need to get out. And the abuser needs to get extensive counseling to change destructive anger patterns, for your sake and the sake of others, because the pattern is often passed from one generation to the next. Most relationships, fortunately, don't experience anger issues to that extreme, but we all sometimes have incorrect tendencies when expressing anger.

After my tour of the Aquarium, it occurred to me that when it comes to processing anger, we act a lot like certain sea creatures. For example, some people are what I call puffer fish. That is, they allow anger to build up inside until they explode. When they do, they feel much better because they've gotten it off their chest, but they've made everyone else feel much worse.

Other people are just the opposite; they're like hermit crabs. They withdraw into their shell when faced with conflict. It seems that with many couples, one is a puffer fish and the other is a hermit crab when it comes to dealing with emotions. One fills up with anger while the other withdraws to avoid conflict.

Then there's the passive-aggressive person I call an angelfish. When I was a kid, I had a fish tank and would save my allowance to buy tropical fish. One day I went to the pet store and saw this big, colorful fish and asked the clerk what kind it was. The store clerk replied, "That's an angelfish." I thought, *How wonderful. It's beautiful and has a great name.* I bought the fish, put it in my tank, and within a few days that angelfish was the only one left. It wasn't as angelic as I thought. It had eaten all the other fish! The angelfish person hides their anger and talks real sweet and angel-like to your face. But their anger comes out behind the scenes through manipulation and gossip.

In fact, it's actually easier to deal with a puffer fish, because at least you know when they are angry. With the passive-aggressive angelfish person, the anger is never out in the open, which makes it hard to confront the real issue. Anger has to come to the surface in order for a relationship to go to new depths.

While I was taking the tour of the Aquarium, I saw an electric eel in a tank by itself. When I asked why, the marine biologist replied, "We can't put that eel with any other fish because it can shock them. In fact, electric eels have such high voltage that in the open sea they've been known to kill divers." Some people are like that electric eel. Nobody wants to be around them because they always seem to be angry and in a bad mood, quick to shock others.

Then you have the shark. The first thing I asked before I did my dive at the Aquarium was, "What about those sharks swimming around?" They said, "Don't worry about the sharks. They've been well fed. The only time you have to worry about the sharks is if you get cut and there's blood in the water." Some people are like those sharks. They attack when there's blood in the water. When they see someone messing up at work, they're all over them in anger. They kind of enjoy conflict. They're pretty good at dominating the ocean of arguments but terrible at building teams.

Finally we have the piranha. At the Aquarium the piranhas looked harmless, but when we dropped some raw chicken into their tank, within a matter of seconds, there were only bits of bone sinking to the bottom. When it comes to processing anger, piranha people gnaw on you with little bites of criticism. Some people don't want to admit that they're angry. They keep their anger hidden under the surface and only allow it to come out in sarcastic cuts. If we were honest, we'd admit that we're all piranha people some of the time, and we, too, have tendencies to gnaw at others with our hidden anger.

Diving Deep

Whatever our anger profile is, for most of us, anger is an awkward thing. Either we live under the false impression that it's sinful to feel anger, or we find ourselves embarrassed and frustrated by our inability to deal with our angry feelings. When you take your awkwardness in dealing with anger and combine it with someone else's—your friend's, family member's, or spouse's anger—you have the potential for damaging the relationships you care about the most.

The problem is that no one teaches us how to express anger and navigate successfully through conflict. Without guidance, many of our relationships will never make it intact.

I don't claim that we can solve all these problems in a day's relationship work, but here are a few ideas regarding anger that might help you. Quite simply, they are *breathe deeply, look and listen,* and *talk honestly.*

Breathe deeply. Because of movies and television, we're all familiar with the advice to count to ten before responding when we're angry. We can practically see the cartoon character counting out the numbers as steam rises and escapes through his ears. Certainly, when anger approaches a flash point—for us or someone else—it's wise to pause to breathe. But perhaps more often in relationships, taking a breath may be about taking a few hours alone to calm down, taking a day to think about things, or taking an afternoon to work out, fix the fence, or go for a walk. Time-out works for adults too.

I think breathing deeply is also about bringing God into the emotions of the moment. Tell God what you feel, and exhale to him your feelings of hurt and anger. It's awkwardly humbling to admit that I can be hurt by someone else, but the quicker I breathe it out to God, the quicker I can inhale his healing.

Look and listen. One of the best pieces of advice I ever heard is that usually the trigger for someone's anger is not the real reason for it. This is obviously true for married couples. Often a trivial thing sparks anger, such as a spouse not taking out the trash or not washing the dishes. Yet the real reason for the anger may be days, months, or even years deeper, such as personal inadequacy, insecurity, grief, stress, or (as we'll discuss later) disappointment that the other person is not meeting one's expectations. In situations of anger and conflict, it's helpful to ask yourself, Why is this really happening? What's behind this outburst? What's the true reason for this anger?

Whether the anger is coming from you or from someone else, it helps if you can step outside of the emotional event—the blowup or the tears—and look and listen for the real cause. Understanding what that might be is critical to moving forward and growing deeper.

When you're in anger situations and you have the insight of distinguishing between the trigger and the cause, it's easier to move beyond the trivial event of the moment. For example, you realize that promising to do better in taking out the trash isn't really the point and won't in itself address the anger at hand.

Talk honestly. One of the frequent mistakes people make in dealing with anger situations is that they say things to calm explosive emotions but fail to speak to real issues. When I say "talk honestly," I'm not referring to saying the right things to smooth over someone else's emotions. Some of us are afraid of emotional outbursts. Since they scare us and threaten our world, it's all too easy for us to offer a quick apology or say a kind word that we really don't mean. But this isn't honest talk.

Honest talk isn't simply nice talk. Often honest talk is messy, difficult, and, yes, awkward. Honest talk allows the expression of true emotions in a relationship, back and forth. It risks talking personally and deeply about underlying causes, fears and insecurities, and unfulfilled expectations.

Likewise, when someone speaks in the heat of anger, much is said that isn't really honest or true. Anger often prompts exaggerations, overstatements, and generalities that may have an element of fact but aren't fully true, such as "You never take out the trash, and you really don't care!" Sometimes the only true element in an angry outburst is the anger itself and the difficult emotions underneath. Saying, "I'm angry," may be stating the obvious, but sometimes it's the most truthful thing that can be said. Honest talk gets beyond both the exaggeration of heated anger and the conciliatory words of appeasement to real, truthful conversation.

How do you talk honestly in anger situations? First, know that emotions really need to be expressed. That's perfectly okay. Anger itself needs to come out, and as awkward and uncomfortable as it may be to receive it, you need to allow it to flow. But after a while, when the emotions have been expressed and the time is right, here are a few powerful words to say: "I would really like for us to try to calm down so we can talk about this."

HOPE AND HEALING IN DEEP WATERS

Some relationships are damaged because of a deep-seated anger that has resulted in harsh words and painful wounds. Over time, these events in a relationship create a kind of hopeless cycle. But I've seen true miracles in relationships, many of which didn't appear to have a shred of hope. While a situation may seem impossible, I believe that with commitment, intention, and God's help, two people can rescue themselves and their relationship from the hurts of the past and discover a miracle.

I promise that if you risk the awkwardness of expressing anger in a productive way, you'll go to a whole new depth in your life and character. If two people can express their anger productively and talk honestly about their conflicts and the root causes, their relationship will grow stronger and thrive.

Dare to step into deeper waters, and let your relationships express themselves fully and honestly.

LASTING LOVE RELATIONSHIP
Challenge

1. Which sea creature best describes your style of expressing anger?
   Which best describes the people in your key relationships? What
   conclusions can you draw from the combination of your style
   and their style? Log on to onemonthtolove.com to get a vivid
   picture of your style of expressing anger.

2. Which deeper cause do you think is most often responsible for
   your anger: hurt, insecurity, stress, grief, feelings of inadequacy,
   or something else?

3. Is there anyone in your life you need to confront? Ask God to
   give you the nerve to risk stepping out and expressing your anger
   productively. Remember, conflict is messy, and you won't do
   everything perfectly, but don't let your imperfections keep you
   from expressing anger and working through it.

Fresh

The Awkwardness of Making Changes

He who rejects change is the architect of decay. The
only human institute which rejects progress is the
cemetery.

HAROLD WILSON

When you're finished changing, you're finished.

BENJAMIN FRANKLIN

hange is inevitable. We change lanes, change clothes, change channels, and
change hairstyles. Not only are things changing around us, but we ourselves
are constantly changing, and so are the people we love. Relationships change over
time; you're always either growing closer or moving further apart. One of the
keys to living an effective life is learning how to adapt to the inevitable changes
that come our way.

We've all heard that change is good for us. But let's be honest. The only
people who really like change are babies with dirty diapers. Instead of looking
for fresh opportunities to grow, most of us stubbornly resist change, sometimes
even preferring pain that's familiar to the fear of uncertainty.

In the early 1900s, the number one horse-and-buggy company in America set a goal: to remain the number one horse-and-buggy company. The trouble was that they didn't see the big picture and anticipate the change that was coming. When a young man named Henry Ford invented the Model T a few years later, they were put out of business. They thought of themselves as a horse-and-buggy company when they should have thought of themselves as a transportation company.

It's easy for us to point out the folly of their decision, but we do the same thing in our relationships all the time. We box our loved ones into narrow roles when we insist on rigidly defining their personalities and potential. We tend to think of our relationships in terms of what they used to be, and that's why we often fail to see ourselves changing, individually and together. It's important to keep the big picture in mind, which means being open to possibilities that are different from who and what we are at this moment.

Love at first sight says, I am who I am, and a relationship that requires me to be different—to change—isn't really worth it. Lasting love says that change is inevitable and important, both for me and for the person I care about. No, it's not easy. Yes, it's sometimes scary. But ultimately it's rewarding, rich, and even fun.

OFF WITH THE OLD

As we grow physically, we have to buy new clothes periodically. Either the old clothes don't fit anymore, they wear out, or they're hopelessly out of style. Our relationships are the same way. Over time we settle into familiar patterns with each other; we wear our same old relationship "outfits." Relationship patterns are fine. There can be rewards and delights in knowing from habit how another person thinks, talks, and responds to certain things. But at some point those patterns can become entrenched. Eventually the old "clothes" start to wear thin until one person or both feel like they're stuck in a rut. So many couples, families, and friendships hobble through life tattered and faded because they're scared to change their relational clothes.

If you've let your relationships fall into the rut of being completely comfortable, you could be in a dangerous place. Someone once said, "A rut is just a grave with both ends knocked out." It is important to feel secure in a relationship, but you shouldn't stop seeking new adventures and activities together. It's essential that you talk about how you want to change and that you agree on some new things you can try together. It may be changing up your daily routine to include a walk together at sunset or a commitment to meet every Tuesday morning for coffee. The point is, you create space in your relationship to anticipate change.

Remember, you are either choosing to grow closer together, or you're drifting apart. We need to constantly grow and make positive changes in our lives and relationships if they're going to be the best they can possibly be.

THREE WINDS OF CHANGE

Change may be something you initiate, something another person initiates that you need to respond to, or a life circumstance you must respond to together. There are three change situations in relationships that we need to be aware of.

Change for change's sake. It seems to me that women are better at this than men. How often do women just get tired of how the house looks and decide to rearrange the furniture, or get frustrated with their wardrobe and buy new clothes? At times we just need to change something in our lives to keep life interesting and to give our personalities room to bloom.

There's a great episode of *The Dick Van Dyke Show* in which Laura Petrie (Mary Tyler Moore) senses that she has become boring to her husband, Rob (Dick Van Dyke). One day while he's away at work, she decides to change her hair from brunette to blond, with the help of her neighbor Millie. As always, stuff happens. Laura runs out of hair color halfway through the job. At the same time, Rob calls and says he's coming home from work early. By the end of the show, Rob walks in the front door, only to find his wife two-toned! Parted exactly in the middle, her hair is half-blond and half-brunette. Through Laura's tears of exasperation, Rob says he loves her just as she is.

The challenge in relationships, of course, is when one person decides to change for change's sake and the other is left behind. As with Rob and Laura, one person might think that the other is bored and that they need to change to keep the relationship exciting. Or conversely, one person might think, *I'm boring to them. They are changing their life because I'm not sufficient.* But healthy relationships accept change in the course of life, no matter who is doing the changing.

While we should never think that making superficial changes to our appearance or to our behavior will make someone truly love us more, making changes to ourselves for the sake of change isn't necessarily a bad thing and can even be healthy. Hopefully this is change that's more significant than Clairol, but it's good sometimes simply to make something different about our everyday lives. It rearranges the furniture of our existence and creates a newness and difference that's refreshing to us and to the people we spend time with.

Change for one's own good. Change to improve ourselves can include going back to school, taking another job, or starting to work out. On another level, this can be dealing with an addiction, going to sessions with a counselor, or developing a deeper relationship with God.

These kinds of life improvements can be threatening to another person. Maybe one of your key relationships is going through a process like this, and you feel insecure. You know they're working to straighten themselves out in one way or another, but you wonder if the person who emerges on the other side of the process will still want you.

In fact, this is precisely the dynamic of codependence in relationships involving addiction. The addict is actually encouraged by the loved one to remain in their destructive or needy behavior patterns, because the relationship has always been based in part on those needs and because both find their significance in those addictive patterns. The challenge is for the enabler in the relationship to encourage and support healthy changes in the other person.

Life stage change. Circumstances of life change us just by the kinds of experiences they bring. A couple is changed by the birth of their child. A man is changed by his marriage to his sweetheart. A young adult is changed by years away at college. Health issues change people, and, of course, the death of a friend or family member can change us profoundly.

How do you feel when your best friend and her husband have a new baby? What happens to someone who depends on you when you get married? As a parent how do you deal with the empty nest when your son leaves for college?

Life happens, change occurs, and relationships can be threatened by it all.

One way of dealing with this is to accept and acknowledge that something is happening and that it needs to be addressed. We often deal with life change by ignoring it and pretending it's not actually happening. It's a lot healthier to acknowledge change and discuss it: "I'm happy for you that you're getting married, but I confess that I feel I'm losing you, and that makes me kind of scared." Also, dealing with life change requires both people in the relationship to be intentional, not about preserving the old patterns of relationship, but about working to create new ones: "I'm excited for you that you're going back to school to finish your degree. I know we'll have less time together, but I'm wondering if we can talk about some new things we can do." Planning together what the changed relationship will look like can go far in reestablishing your connection on new ground.

Whether in a friendship, a marriage, a sibling relationship, or a parent-child relationship, it's critical that you both acknowledge the changes that will occur or already are happening. Talk together about what that means and how it feels.

SET YOUR SAILS

You can't control the unexpected changes that enter your life, but you can choose to adapt to them. If you don't set your sails to catch the winds of change, your relationship will eventually be torn apart by them. The first step to adapting to changes that blow into our lives is learning to see them in a different way.

The apostle Paul, in 2 Corinthians 12:7, talks about what he thought was a devastating change that came into his life, a "thorn in my flesh." He never reveals what it was, but some scholars speculate it could have been that his eyesight began to fail, which would have made writing difficult. We don't know what the painful change was that Paul was dealing with, but we do know he prayed three times for God to take it away. God, however, didn't change the situation; he changed Paul *in* the situation. Paul would later say, "At first I didn't think of it as a gift, and begged God to remove it.… And then he told me, 'My grace is enough; it's all you need. My strength comes into its own in your weakness.' Once I heard that, I…began appreciating the gift" (12:8–9, MSG).

To adapt to change, we need to be like Paul and come to see change as a gift rather than a problem. If we're always focusing on the negative aspects of the changes that come into our lives, we'll continually be stuck in self-pity, and our relationships will suffer.

In 2004, to celebrate the first show of her nineteenth season on the air, Oprah Winfrey gave everyone in her audience that day a brand-new car: 276 brand-new Pontiac G6s. The audience went crazy, jumping up and down in excitement over the unexpected, amazing gift.

A year later some of them weren't jumping up and down anymore as the IRS came down on them for not paying up to seven thousand dollars in the gift taxes they owed. Some things that come into our lives appear to be exciting, wonderful gifts, but a few years down the road, we discover they weren't all they were cracked up to be.

Conversely, some of the greatest gifts that come into our lives are things we don't recognize as gifts at first. In fact, many times what we see as our greatest problem often turns out to be a great gift. Cancer is not good. It is a terrible disease. But I've seen many people undergo cancer surgery and treatment and say that, in spite of the fear, uncertainty, and pain, they now see all they've gone through as a gift. Their families are closer than ever, and their relationship with God has grown deeper and stronger.

Losing your job is not good, but I've talked to so many people who have told me, "I didn't see it at the time, but losing my job was the best thing that could've happened to me because it changed my whole direction. I wouldn't be where I am now if it hadn't happened."

Divorce is not good, but I was talking to a friend recently who said, "When my spouse left me, I was devastated, but that's when my relationship with God became real."

When difficult and painful changes come into our lives, it's almost impossible to see them as gifts at the time. We have to choose, however, to stop dwelling on the past and to catch the winds of change so we can sail into a positive future.

THE ONLY UNCHANGEABLE

Change is important and worth doing, but it sure can be messy. You work hard to get relationships going well on one level, and then you realize one of you is going to change. Not only do you have to reapply all the relationship skills you've been learning to a whole new situation, but you start to realize that change is constant and that relationships have to be worked on and mastered on the fly. Indeed, change is a mess…but a mess worth making. When others in our relationships change, it can feel awkward to talk about it, but the risk of addressing it is critical. Change will happen in life—that's a fact. Being able to accommodate those changes and work together to deepen and grow our relationships is what true lasting love is about.

It's great to know that when everything is shifting in and around us, we have a heavenly Father who never changes. God assures us, "I am the LORD, and I do not change" (Malachi 3:6, NLT). You can always count on him, because he *never* changes. God's Word never changes either. The Bible tells us "The grass withers and the flowers fall, but the word of our God stands forever" (Isaiah 40:8).

The two of us decided to build our lives on Christ and his Word, and after we made that one decision, all the other decisions in life got a lot easier. Once you decide what never changes, then you have the flexibility and freedom to change everything else.

LASTING LOVE RELATIONSHIP
Challenge

1. Think about the key relationships in your life. What changes are they going through? Can you anticipate other changes that are coming? Record your thoughts and feelings in your journal.

2. Do you feel that any of your key relationships are in a rut? What might you do with them to "rearrange the furniture"?

3. Choose to focus on a key relationship this week, and dare to talk about the change that one of you is going through.

Better Together

The Awkwardness of Unity

A marriage made in heaven is one where a man and a woman become more richly themselves together than the chances are either of them could ever have managed to become alone.

FREDERICK BUECHNER

Love does not consist in gazing at each other but in looking outward together in the same direction.

ANTOINE DE SAINT-EXUPÉRY

We believe it is much harder to write a book together than it would be to write one individually. It takes extra time and work to communicate our ideas to each other and make sure we're on the same page before the writing begins. Yet we love to write as coauthors for one reason: we're much better together.

It's also harder for us to do public speaking together than separately. We often struggle putting together our talks because we have unique personalities and communication styles that often clash in the preparation stage. However, we love to speak together for one reason: we're much better together.

True relationships—whether best friends, brothers, sisters, parent-child, or a husband and wife—find deep meaning and purpose in acts of teamwork. Their unique chemistry works together to create something remarkable. When this happens, not only are two people better together, but they are also sharing something they would otherwise miss out on: a oneness of creativity, purpose, and spirit. The power of two can accomplish great things.

THE POWER OF TWO

Here's the story of two guys. They met in high school. They connected with each other, as they later joked, because they were both misfits. In gym class the two overweight boys were forced to run track, and that disastrous experience likely cemented their early friendship. They both graduated high school in the late sixties and launched themselves into…failure. One found himself being fired from a series of jobs. The other dreamed of going to medical school and failed to get admitted (twice).

One was especially artistic; the other was seriously interested in helping people. Different, but similar in spirit, they began to explore a common dream. The thing was, they both loved food.

Together they took a course in food preparation, a correspondence course that cost them each a total of five dollars. Not long after that, they joined forces to open their first shop in a run-down garage. In time the little shop became very popular in their hometown, and soon it was the talk of their state and their region.

The rest is history—and the power of two.

Today Ben Cohen and Jerry Greenfield are running an ice-cream empire that combines creative flavors and names (like Cherry Garcia and Chunky Monkey) with mission-oriented values that help people (including charitable programs that support small businesses). The two were even named U.S. Small Business Persons of the Year in a ceremony hosted by President Reagan in 1988.

Ben and Jerry are a great example of two misfits with different skills and abilities who teamed up to accomplish great things. You, too, can find this kind of teamwork with your key relationships. You may not start an ice-cream empire, but how big or commercially successful the result is doesn't really matter. The question is, what can the two of you do together that you can't do on your own? The challenge is to dare to explore such things, talk about them together, and overcome awkwardness in working together toward a common goal.

Strengths and Weaknesses

They say the true test of a relationship is to hang wallpaper together. Wallpaper hanging appears to be simple and straightforward on the surface, but in reality it's complicated enough to drive two people crazy. When you think about it, it's a job that's nearly impossible for a person to do alone. One has to stand on a ladder and position the sheet of wallpaper. The other has to stand back and direct: "An inch to the left. No, it's crooked. There. Now bring it down farther…" If the one on the ladder isn't good at spatial skills or doesn't know how wide an inch is, and if the one standing back isn't good at communicating clearly, the project winds up a mess.

The secret to a great partnership, whether it's a husband-and-wife team or two best friends in tandem, is learning how to complement each other's strengths and weaknesses. It may be hard for one of you to admit aloud, "You're better at this than I am," but when both people get to that point, it's the beginning of something great. We're always better together, because no one has every strength, and everyone has many weaknesses.

Early in any relationship, all we tend to see are the other person's strengths, and we're usually blind to their weaknesses. This is love at *first* sight. We may even have illusions that we are great partners solely because we're so enamored with each other and because we desperately want to believe we're perfect together. Of course, the problem is that we haven't actually done anything together yet.

Partnering with another person and finding true unity of heart and spirit starts with a clear understanding of each other's strengths (even when they compete with our own) and personal weaknesses. This is lasting love—honest, clear, transparent acknowledgment of the truth about ourselves and each other and then fitting those strengths and weaknesses together to complete a beautiful puzzle that makes us better together.

Most of the time we simply don't work at this nearly enough.

John Ortberg says the problem for many married couples is that they have the wrong concept of a relationship. He says that most people think marriage is like buying a new car. It's good to begin with, but it goes bad over time.

Think about it. When you buy a new car, it looks great. It drives great. It even smells great. I love that new-car smell. Unfortunately, in our family the new-car smell doesn't last long. It's quickly replaced by the old-chicken-nugget-under-the-seat smell.

But all new cars eventually lose their luster. They get a few dings and scratches. The engine starts to have some trouble, and the new-car smell eventually fades. Some couples who have this concept of marriage try to get it back to the way it was at first, because they mistakenly believe that, like a new car, everything was perfect at the beginning of the relationship. Of course, that never works. It's like when I use the new-car-smell air freshener in my old car. It just ends up smelling like new-car air freshener trying to cover up the old-chicken-nugget-under-the-seat smell.

Too often people say, "I'll just trade in my spouse for a new model," and they exchange their relationship for a new one and start the process all over again. Lasting love says that relationships have to be worked at. It takes time, conversation, and shared experiences to come to a mutual understanding of each other's strengths and weaknesses. Ultimately, the relationship may never have that new-car smell again, but it will develop a great new fragrance resulting from the chemistry of two people working together beautifully.

The true image—the biblical image—of relationships is nothing like a new car but rather two boxes of broken pieces. Each of us is pretty much a mess of brokenness, but when we begin to admit our weaknesses and match up spare parts, we have the beginning of something beautiful.

ONE PURPOSE

The Bible says, "[Be] of the same mind, maintaining the same love, united in spirit, intent on one purpose" (Philippians 2:2, NASB). In relationships the goal is to acknowledge how different we are in our personalities, strengths, and weaknesses and yet remain one in purpose.

A simple exercise you might do together requires you to be a talent scout. Sit down with each other, and take turns making a simple statement of something—a skill, ability, talent—that you think the other is gifted with. Write down the lists, and after you have several things for each of you, spend time talking about them. Look for pairs of strengths, and brainstorm what sort of activity or project that talent pair might lead you to do together. For example, if one of you is good at gardening and the other is skilled in building things, what project might you do together that employs both of those skills?

Sometimes we limit the possibilities of our teamwork to personal interests, hobbies, and sports activities. But one of the most rewarding activities that people can partner in is service. There is something powerful about uniting for a purpose that is greater than ourselves. Nothing brings two people together more quickly or closely than using their gifts and strengths for a purpose that glorifies God and makes a difference in the lives of others.

It is so important to get involved in serving others in some aspect of your lives together. Ask each other what your life mission together might be. Have you ever talked that way, exploring what your lives might jointly create that could help people in some greater way than either of you could accomplish individually? What could you be involved in that will outlast you both?

THE WORK IS WORTH IT

Whether it's being unified in your commitment to the relationship, building oneness by serving, or sharing an activity together, it will take a conscious effort to overcome the awkwardness you feel about approaching each other in this area. It's always easier to do things on your own, but if you're not careful, the path of least resistance will separate you over time.

I've seen many marriages drift apart because the husband and wife never made an intentional effort to do life together. They each developed their own hobbies, interests, and sets of friends, and they never sought to do anything together as a team. We speak from experience when we say there is nothing more rewarding than sharing life together. We love to parent together, write books together, speak together, and serve others together. Though it's not always easy, and we sometimes get frustrated with each other because of our differences and weaknesses, we are most definitely *better together.*

LASTING LOVE RELATIONSHIP
Challenge ⎯⎯⎯⎯⎯⎯⎯⎯⎯

1. Consider your key relationships. Could you plan a conversation with one of them about teaming up to do or create something? Go to onemonthtolove.com and hear us talk candidly about how we work together.
2. Try the talent scout exercise. See what mutual activities or projects might come out of pairing up the talents on the lists.
3. Is there a service opportunity you could do together? Spend some time together to explore your ideas. What steps do you need to take to make that a reality?

THE ART OF LETTING GO

Remote Control

Practicing the Art of Letting Go

> The way to love anything is to realize that it might
> be lost.
>
> G. K. CHESTERTON

> Love does not dominate; it cultivates.
>
> JOHANN WOLFGANG VON GOETHE

Did you see the movie *Click* that came out a few years ago? Adam Sandler plays Michael Newman, who receives the ultimate remote-control device—one that allows him to control his personal universe, including muting, skipping, and dubbing his life. Not only can he skip over every argument or negative situation, but he can also fast-forward to the best parts of his life: promotions, celebrations, and vacations. Sounds good, doesn't it?

A fantasy, for sure, but in many ways we all attempt to re-create the same thing in our relationships. We seek to control our lives and the lives of others to make ourselves feel more secure and important. Many of us don't realize we do this. We employ these controlling behaviors and strategies so quietly and invisibly that we're blind to them. Yet we push people's buttons to create the experiences and relationships that serve our purposes.

There are many ways we seek to control others. Some of us are perfectionists, seeking control by imposing impossible standards on everything and everyone. By doing so, perfectionists establish that they are the best. The problem is
that this also implies that no one else is good enough.

Other people are intimidators. Intimidators use threats, demands, angry
outbursts, and sarcasm to take control of people and situations. Of course, as
they grab control, they also drive people away.

Some of us control through worry and anxiety. Worrywarts gain control
by assuming there's always something else to be checked, rechecked, and triple-
checked. No one else, they say, is careful enough, and only the worrywart is
truly taking charge in the safest way.

Many people control through constant planning. Planners establish schedules, agendas, sequences, and routines for themselves and everyone else. When
there is a deviation from the plan, the planner declares that something is wrong
or off schedule, thereby gaining a measure of power and control.

The micromanager controls through an obsession with detail. By making
the smallest details the most important things, they try to make themselves important. They also frustrate other people to no end.

These are just a few of the many different ways we devise to remotely control the world around us, often including our key relationships. But why do we
seek to control? Where does this desire come from? No doubt it derives from
core issues in our lives, struggles we have with deep feelings of inadequacy, pain,
and fear. We seek to control because otherwise we are scared we won't measure
up or be accepted.

There are six core issues that seem to be the most common: hurt, insecurity, pride, guilt, selfishness, and unrealistic expectations. Over the next week
we'll explore how our struggle in each area can create a desire to seek control over
our own lives and the lives of others. We'll examine how these core issues can
result in controlling behaviors that threaten and sabotage our key relationships.

The bottom line is that we all struggle with control issues. Control is all about trying to remove the unknown. It keeps us from trusting others and trusting God. The upside-down thinking of the world says, "The unknown is scary. I don't know who I can trust. If I take matters into my own hands, if I control things, I can eliminate the fear of the unknown." But right-side-up wisdom says, "The unknown is a place of trust. Perfect love casts out all fear. Only when I release control and trust God can I experience real love."

Jesus demonstrated that we have to pursue the art of letting go if we want to experience lasting love. The Bible shows Jesus taking his disciples through the painful and yet rewarding process of letting go. Simon Peter and his partners were trying to control their fishing business, but they ran into some circumstances that were way beyond their control. After a long, unproductive night of fishing, Peter said, "Master, we've worked hard all night and haven't caught anything" (Luke 5:5). You can just hear the frustration in that statement. Their whole livelihood depended on their catch. Since they couldn't control it, they were frustrated.

It's so discouraging trying to control your problems and other people when neither will cooperate. It also wears you out. These guys had worked hard all night. In the original Greek, the word *kopiao* is used, which literally means "to be wearied or fatigued." Peter was saying, "We are worn out. We're beat. We're toast. Stick a fork in us; we're done." It's exhausting to try to be the general manager of the universe and the glue that keeps it all together.

Trying to be in control is also a losing proposition. Peter said, "We haven't caught anything." They had failed miserably and completely. Trying to control always ends in failure because trying to control is really trying to play God. There's only one God, and you're not him!

Many relationships end in failure because of control issues. Some people think they're doing the most loving thing when they hold on to a relationship too tightly. The reality is that holding on too tightly will eventually crush the life and love out of it. That's because it usually has more to do with a fear of losing the relationship than it does with wanting the best for the other person.

Lasting love is as much about what you let go of as it is about what you add to your relationships. When you start practicing the art of letting go, a weight begins to lift, and that gives both of you the freedom to grow.

Raising the White Flag

Simon Peter's fishing story also shows us the process for letting go of control. It's a process that leads to life, freedom, peace, and blessing. And it all starts by giving up.

Peter and his friends had tried hard but came to realize that the circumstances were beyond their control. Ultimately they just flat-out gave up, and that's when Jesus entered the story. When we come to the place where we say, "I give up. I can't control this situation," or, "I just can't fix this relationship," then God enters the scene of our lives. Once we stop trying to fix the problem, change the person, or control the situation, then God can get involved.

But there's more. After we give up control, we have to give *over* control. We often drive our lives the way we drive our cars. We white-knuckle the steering wheel, driving for hours upon end and taking so many wrong turns that we're lost, worn-out, frustrated, and exhausted. We want to give up, but we're afraid that if we let go of the wheel, we'll crash. That's why we can't just *give up*. We have to *give over* control to someone else.

Jesus said to Peter, "Hey, why don't you go out to the deep water and throw your nets out for a catch?" I'm sure Peter was thinking, *Jesus, you're great at this spiritual stuff, but fishing is* my *gig. I'm the expert here. Besides, everyone knows that, in the Sea of Galilee, you catch fish in the shallow water at night—not in deep water in the heat of the day.* But out of respect for Jesus, Peter acquiesced. He complained about it a little, saying, "Master, we've worked hard all night, and we haven't caught anything. We know what we're doing here, so I don't know why we'd want to cast our nets out again in the deep in the heat of the day, but if you say so, we'll do it."

And you know what happened? The nets were so full of fish that they practically burst. I'm sure it was the single largest catch of their entire lives.

The question is, why did Jesus perform this miracle? It's not like he was healing a sick person or raising someone from the dead. Why in the world did Jesus perform a miracle where he just *gave* Peter a boatload of fish? Well, Jesus wanted Peter to understand that he could give over control of every area of his life. And he wants you to see that you can give over control of every area of your life today too.

Really, we have to give Peter some credit here, because at least he obeyed. He didn't understand it, and he certainly didn't feel like it, but he did it. I think he obeyed because he had given up. He had tried everything else, and nothing was working.

So when everything else isn't working, why not give Jesus a try? Why not give it over to God? Look at what happened to Peter when he surrendered—Jesus worked a miracle. The Bible says that "all his companions were astonished at the catch of fish they had taken" (Luke 5:9). Don't you just love that word *astonished*? God loves to astonish his children with miracles and blessings when they trust him, and he wants to astonish you by showing that he cares about every area of your life, including that relationship you've been trying to control.

God wants to astonish you in how he can work with you in your key relationships. The thing is, we tend to mess up our relationships because we try to fix them on our own. We need to understand that our strategies to control our lives and the lives of others are misguided and harmful. They're motivated by our own private struggles with hurt, insecurity, pride, guilt, selfishness, and unrealistic expectations. God wants to teach us what he taught Peter. He wants us to experience the peace that comes from giving over control.

This is the art of letting go.

LASTING LOVE RELATIONSHIP
Challenge

1. Of the types of remote-control methods we mentioned, which type do you identify with? Do others control you in one of those ways? How do you feel when someone tries to control you?

2. Of your key relationships, which do you seek to control, either quietly or overtly?

3. Of the six core issues we mentioned (hurt, insecurity, pride, guilt, selfishness, and unrealistic expectations), which ring true for you?

The Spear

Letting Go of Hurt

I have decided to stick with love. Hate is too great a
burden to bear.

MARTIN LUTHER KING JR.

Getting over a painful experience is much like crossing
monkey bars. You have to let go at some point in order
to move forward.

ANONYMOUS

In the 1950s the most vicious and violent society on the face of the earth was
the Waodani tribe, who lived in the rain forest of Ecuador. The Waodani had
a culture of revenge that had been passed down for generations. If someone in
the tribe wronged you in any way, you had the right to spear them. It was that
simple. The Waodani people were killing each other at such an incredible rate
that by 1955 they were almost extinct.

From the outside, this culture of revenge is difficult to comprehend. It seems
insane to murder someone just because they offended you. But if you think
about it, our "civilized" culture is really just as bizarre underneath its plastic, po-
lite veneer. Maybe we don't spear people physically, but we use emotional spears.

Granted, the offense isn't that someone poached on our hunting ground, but our relationships are constantly pierced by what someone else has done to us or by what we perceive has been done to us.

So many relationships are sabotaged by unspoken, unresolved resentments. Sometimes people aren't even aware they've inflicted harm on each other. Sometimes wounds are accidental but are believed to have been intentional. And, of course, many times we do intentionally wrong each other.

In relationships, two things are at work here: the hurts themselves, which often go unaddressed and unresolved, and also resentment, the resulting deep-seated turmoil that ultimately infects and destroys.

THE END OF THE SPEAR

In 1956 five American missionaries, led by missionary pilot Nate Saint, flew a little plane into the jungles of Ecuador and landed on a beach in the Amazon River basin. They had been planning for months, even years, to reach out to the Waodani tribe and share the love of Christ in hopes they could help change the tribe's violent ways. The missionaries knew it was a great risk, but they felt God's calling on their lives to go.

Their first meeting was a success. They made contact with the tribe, and the Waodani seemed to accept them. The tribesmen were as curious about the Americans' airplane as they were intrigued by the foreigners themselves.

But the second meeting took a tragic turn. In a vicious massacre, all five missionaries were speared. The story made the cover of all the national newsmagazines and became one of the significant international stories of the decade. It remains one of the most quoted accounts in missionary history.

One of the reasons this was such a notable event is that the missionaries' deaths weren't the end of the story. What happened next was a radical display of astounding forgiveness.

Several of the widowed missionary wives actually went to live with the

Waodani people. Can you imagine that? These warriors had killed their husbands, and the women went back into those killing grounds to live among them! At first the Waodani threatened to kill the women just as they had killed their husbands. But then, perhaps because they were women, the tribe accepted them and allowed them to stay. The missionary wives began to share the love of Christ, and over time the culture of revenge was transformed into a culture of love, peace, and hope.

The movie *End of the Spear* recounts this story, but it also depicts the life of Steve Saint, Nate Saint's son, who grew up with the Waodani people. Steve witnessed the people who had killed his father turn to Christ and drop their spears of revenge.

When Steve arrived in Ecuador as a young boy, he didn't have the skills necessary to live in the jungle. Since he didn't know how to hunt or fend for himself, one of the Waodani, a warrior named Mincaye, offered to take him under his wing and teach him the skills he needed to survive.

What was remarkable was that Mincaye was the very one who had speared Steve's father.

An incredible bond formed between the two. They both took a risk, and they both had to learn to trust. According to Waodani culture, Steve Saint had a right to kill Mincaye, and Mincaye was teaching him the skills he could use to do so if he chose.

There's a scene in the movie where Steve, as a grown man, walks down to the beach on the banks of the Amazon River with Mincaye. As Mincaye shows Steve the place where he speared his father, we can sense the bitterness and resentment beginning to well up in Steve's heart. But it is there on the beach, the very spot where his father was killed, that Steve finally lets go of his last spear of resentment. He knows that his father chose to come to this place, fully aware that it could cost him his life, because he wanted to share the gospel with the Waodani. Steve begins to see the Waodani as the most special people on earth precisely because his father was willing to die for them.

GOD WRITES THE STORY

A few years ago I had the privilege of interviewing Steve Saint and Mincaye. Mincaye is now a great man of God, and the two are close friends. In fact, Steve calls Mincaye "grandfather," and Mincaye calls Steve "baba," which means "son." It's amazing to see the love they now share.

In my conversation with Steve, he made a profound comment: "When God writes our story, he doesn't promise us that all the chapters will be easy. The good news is that if we let God write our story, when those bad chapters come, the hope we have is that in the last chapter, he promises us that he will make sense of all those other chapters."

What a beautiful picture of forgiveness: letting go and choosing to let God write our story.

So often in relationships we want to write our own story. We try to control how things begin, how they develop, and how they end. And we especially enjoy writing a story that rights the wrongs that have been done to us.

Maybe you've been holding on to a spear of resentment for a long time. Maybe someone wounded you deeply, and you are now reaching for that spear. It's time to recognize that this will destroy you and hold you back from experiencing healing in your life. God has so much more in store for your future if you will release the spear of resentment and allow him to write your story. He saw what happened, and he cries with you. He didn't bring that destruction into your life, but he can turn it around if you'll let him.

DROPPING THE SPEAR

But how do you do it? How do you release the spear of resentment? First, you have to admit your hurt and bitterness. Many times we simply aren't honest with ourselves about what we have experienced and how we feel. Or we may try to pretend that we are strong or superspiritual by hiding our hurts.

Until you acknowledge the hurts you feel, you can't progress beyond them. When you stuff your anger and hold on to your hurt, you think it's under control, but really it leaks out and begins poisoning your relationship with toxins of bitterness.

So name it—name the hurt you feel. Let it out. Speak it aloud. Write it in your journal. Accept that you've been hurt and that this needs to be dealt with.

Second, you must tell the person who hurt you. This will probably be difficult to do, which is likely why you've avoided it. But it's important, even essential, to your relationship to let them in on what you are harboring against them. It's obvious, but we often forget that a relationship is two-way. How can a relationship grow if the other person doesn't know what you're feeling? You could begin the conversation by saying, "Something you did hurt me. Can we talk about it?"

Many times a person who truly loves you will respond with concern and want to know what they did to offend or hurt. But be prepared for any number of other responses: "I didn't say that," or, "I don't recall doing that," or, "You were offended by that little thing?" Remember that the purpose of talking about your hurt to the other person isn't necessarily to reach agreement, settle an argument, or get an apology. The goal is for you to release your hurt openly and to communicate what happened. There's great healing simply in the process of doing that.

Third, you need to forgive. This is the only way to truly release resentment. All relationships encounter hurts, but great relationships address them openly and are built on honest, genuine forgiveness.

Letting go of the hurt doesn't mean you dismiss what happened and make light of it. Forgiveness is not saying, "Oh, don't worry about it. It's not a big deal. I forgive you," when in fact it is a big deal. Forgiveness is being gut-level honest. It says, "What you did hurt me deeply, but I choose to forgive you with God's power." Letting go doesn't mean ignoring the hurt; it means opening the door for healing.

There's a passage in Scripture where Jesus says, "If you see your friend going wrong, correct him. If he responds, forgive him. Even if it's personal against you and repeated seven times through the day, and seven times he says, 'I'm sorry, I won't do it again,' forgive him" (Luke 17:3–4, MSG).

The disciples responded, "Well, you're going to have to give us more faith because we can't do that" (see verse 5). And that's the whole point. It's not about us, and it's not about our feelings. Jesus was saying that we need to choose to forgive as many times as it takes for the memory of the pain to fade away.

There may be someone who hurt you in the past who is no longer in your life. Sometimes it's not appropriate or even possible to go to them to express forgiveness, but it's still essential to choose to forgive them. That's because you forgive for your own sake; otherwise the bitterness you hold on to will affect your present relationships.

It's also important to remember that when you forgive someone, it doesn't mean you should put yourself right back in a situation where they will likely hurt you again. Forgiveness is something you choose to do instantly, but trust is something that takes time to rebuild. For instance, let's say you had a business partner who cheated you. God commands you to choose to forgive that person for your own sake and the sake of your relationship. He doesn't command you, however, to go back into business with your former partner.

Fourth, you need to give your hurt over to God. One of the things I do when someone hurts me is to pray, *God, I choose to forgive by your power even though I don't feel like it.* Later, when the memory comes back, I pray that again. I find that by repeatedly bringing it to God, true healing begins to take place.

TRUE FORGIVENESS

A few years ago our friend Terrilynn went through a terrible tragedy when her twenty-two-year-old son was murdered at college. One of the young men who was involved in the murder was convicted and about to be sentenced. Just before the sentencing date, Terrilynn had been doing the One-Month-to-Live Challenge based on our book *One Month to Live*. Despite her grief, she came to a conviction: "If I had only one month to live, I would want to forgive everyone, including my son's murderer."

When the time came for the ruling, the judge asked Terrilynn if she wanted to say anything to the man who was involved in her son's murder. She stood up in the courtroom and read aloud the most beautiful letter of forgiveness. She looked at the young man who took her son's life and said, "I choose to forgive you for my own healing because I see Jesus standing next to you, begging me to forgive you. And if you become a saver of lives instead of a destroyer of lives, then maybe my son's death won't be in vain."

The judge was stunned. He asked if he could have a copy of her letter and said that in all his years on the bench, he had never heard such a powerful statement.

The young man broke down in tears and said he wanted to hug Terrilynn. She soon began to visit him in prison and mentor him. Over time he made a faith commitment to Christ and today is growing in his new walk with God.

One day I asked Terrilynn, "How were you able to forgive him?"

She replied honestly, "I didn't know if I would be able to do it, but when I stood up in the courtroom, God gave me the strength."

If God can give Terrilynn the strength to forgive her son's murderer, then he can give you the strength to forgive and let go of your hurts so you can embrace his healing. If he can give Steve Saint and the wives of those faithful missionaries the strength to release their spears of resentment so that an entire tribe of people could experience healing and a new path, he can give you the strength to put down your spears so you can experience lasting love.

LASTING LOVE RELATIONSHIP
Challenge _____

1. Think about your key relationships. Is one or more of them affected by a hurt you've experienced from them?
2. Have you thought about the possibility that something *you* did or said has hurt *them*? What might that have been?
3. Consider how you could speak to them about the hurt you feel. Plan to have that conversation soon.

People Pleaser

Letting Go of Insecurity

> I don't know the key to success, but the key to failure is
> trying to please everyone.
>
> BILL COSBY

> Nothing can bring a real sense of security into the
> home except true love.
>
> BILLY GRAHAM

I admit it. I'm a recovering people pleaser. I don't like to disappoint anyone, much less the people closest to me. I used to think that trying to please everyone in my life was a good thing, even a godly thing. I've since seen my people-pleasing tendency cause too much pain in my relationships and in my own life to think it's anything but destructive.

And it's not only destructive—it's impossible! Trying to please everyone always ends in failure. Even God can't please everyone. When God brings rain, some people are really happy because their yard needed it desperately, but the folks who planned outdoor activities are really upset. Why do we try to do what even God can't do?

LOVING VERSUS PLEASING

The root cause of people-pleasing tendencies is the same core issue found in almost all relational problems: insecurity.

Beth Moore, in her book *So Long, Insecurity,* writes, "We all have insecurities. They piggyback on the vulnerability inherent in our humanity. The question is whether or not our insecurities are substantial enough to hurt, limit, or even distract us from profound effectiveness or fulfillment of purpose."[11] We try to please people because we're afraid that if we're honest and share our true selves, they may not like us. They may disapprove of us. They may reject us. *We may be seen as inadequate.*

So we hide behind our fake smiles and wear our masks. We strive to manipulate circumstances and contort our actions, thoughts, and words to keep someone else happy. But what's really happening is that our deep insecurities make our connections with others artificial. If you long for rich, authentic relationships, you have to let go of the insecurities that push you into people pleasing.

INSECURITIES AS CRUTCHES

The Bible tells about the early years of Moses' life. He was destined to be the next pharaoh of Egypt, but because of failures in his life, he ended up in the desert, tending sheep. He had lost everything. Well, almost everything. He still had an old crooked stick, a staff he used to corral the sheep.

God spoke to him and asked, "What's that you hold in your hand, Moses?"

"It's just my shepherd's staff," Moses replied.

"Moses, throw it down on the ground" (see Exodus 4:2–3).

I'm sure Moses was thinking, *It's just an old stick. It's no big deal.* But God knew that, to Moses, the staff represented all he had left in the world. His livelihood and his security were tied up in that simple shepherd's staff. God was telling Moses, "If it's no big deal, throw it down and give it to me." God wanted to teach Moses that he could trust God with everything. He was saying, "Let go and trust me alone." He wanted Moses to release his insecurity so he could use Moses in a mighty way.

God asks us the same question today: "What's that in your hand? What are you holding on to and afraid to let go of?" Is it a relationship you're holding too tightly and trying to control? Is it a loved one you're trying to change? Is it a friendship you're worried about? Is it a relationship with a family member that you're trying to fix? Is it your own insecurity? your own fear?

Until you let go of your insecurity, you will always struggle with trying to earn the approval of the people in your life.

When Moses let go of his shepherd's staff, it changed everything. God gave his staff back to him, but it was no longer an old shepherd's staff. It was completely different. Oh, it looked just the same, but it was now the mighty rod of God and would become the powerful symbol of his power. It was this staff that Moses would later hold over the Red Sea to make it part down the middle, a miracle that would save an entire people. That surrendered shepherd's staff was what God used over and over again to perform miracles for the people of Israel.

Before he gave it to God, Moses' shepherd's staff was his crutch, his false security. For many of us, our crutch is people pleasing. But it, like Moses' staff, is a falsehood, propping us up against our inner insecurities.

When you let go of your crutches, God will transform your life and relationships. After all, there is only One whom we should seek to please. Colossians 3:23 says, "Whatever you do, work at it with all your heart, as working for the Lord." When I focus on pleasing God, he fills me with passion so I can put all my heart into whatever I'm doing. If I live my life for the One who created me and died for me, all my insecurities will fade, and every particle of fear will fall away.

AUDIENCE OF ONE

One of my favorite movies is *Gladiator*. I don't condone the violence, but the story is powerful. The reason the movie really grabs my heart is because of the character played by Russell Crowe—Maximus.

If you know the story, you know that Maximus was a great general of Rome, a man of integrity. Maximus loved his family with all his heart, and he loved the men who served him with all his heart. As a result, they respected him, loved him, and would have gladly given their lives for him. The movie depicts how the jealous emperor had Maximus's family killed. Maximus became a slave who gradually rose to the rank of gladiator. Then unfolds an extraordinary story of courage and integrity.

All the other gladiators wanted to please the emperor so they would be released. In the Colosseum arena, after a gladiator knocked down his opponent, he would look to the emperor. The emperor would give a signal to indicate if he wanted the gladiator to kill his opponent or let him live to fight another day. The emperor would usually listen to the cheers of the crowd and make his decision based on what pleased them. Essentially, the whim of the crowd ultimately determined the poor man's fate.

But Maximus had no desire to please the crowd or the emperor or even to ensure his own personal welfare. He couldn't care less about pleasing anyone. Maximus had no fear of people and no fear of death, because he loved something more than his own life. He loved the family he had lost, and he loved Rome and wanted it to return to its original glory. The strange thing is, when Maximus refused to follow the crowd's wishes and defied the emperor, everyone in the Colosseum sat in stunned silence. Then the crowd started to chant, "Maximus! Maximus! Maximus!" as the jealous emperor looked on in disbelief.

Doesn't something about the crowd's reaction resonate within you? When we see someone acting out of integrity and love for others, without regard for what people think of them, it takes us by surprise and fills us with respect and admiration.

I want to be like Maximus in my relationships. I want to love God and others more than my own comfort, to care more about loving people than what people think of me. And with God's help, I'm learning to look to the One who loved me more than his own comfort, the One who loved me enough to go to the cross instead of pleasing the crowd.

When I seek to please the God who created me, it's as if the crowd fades away and all that's left is the audience of One.

PEOPLE PLEASING UPSIDE DOWN

What has helped me as a recovering people pleaser is the realization that pleasing people isn't loving at all. It's really just a cover-up of our own insecurities and, at its core, a selfish act. It's protecting ourselves at the expense of the relationship. People pleasing is actually one of the most unloving ways you can relate to others, because you avoid sharing your true self with them. It's also incredibly condescending toward the other person. Essentially we're saying, "You can't handle this on your own. Let me smooth it over for you." In a real way, it's a form of dishonesty.

What's more, people pleasing is an expression of distrust and a lack of confidence. For example, when I try to please my spouse (because I fear revealing my true feelings), I'm really saying, "I don't trust or love you enough to be honest." When I try to please a friend because I'm afraid of losing the friendship, I'm basically saying, "I don't value our friendship enough to be myself with you."

Letting go of the insecurities that breed the behavior of people pleasing is really a decision to pursue honest, real relationships. It's a commitment to relate to another person on an even playing field, sharing the truth of life together.

MY JOURNEY AND YOURS

For me it's a daily struggle. I am still inclined to people please. It's hard for me even now to let go of my insecurities enough to be perfectly authentic. But I'm learning. One verse that speaks powerfully to me about this is 1 John 4:18: "Fully-developed love expels every particle of fear" (Phillips). The opposite of in-security is not faith and courage but love. When unconditional love and com-mitment are the foundation of a relationship, it motivates you to let go of fear and enables you to express yourself openly and honestly.

When I realize how much God loves me, it frees me to let go of what peo-ple think about me. This has been one of the most amazing truths I've ever ex-perienced. I have finally come to the place where I ask God's forgiveness for trying to please people instead of really loving them.

Not only is this freeing; it's also relaxing. People pleasing is a lot of work! It will wear you out. Letting go is, in addition to everything else, a great relief.

LASTING LOVE RELATIONSHIP
Challenge

1. Can you think of a key relationship in which you've been more concerned about keeping them happy than being honest with them? What kinds of behaviors do you engage in while trying to please? What are some consequences you've experienced?

2. The root cause of people pleasing is insecurity. What are you insecure about in your most important relationships? Write them down in your journal.

3. Memorize 1 John 4:18. Realize that God's unconditional love frees you to risk loving whether you please the person or not.

Ego Trip

Letting Go of Pride

Of the billionaires I have known, money just brings
out the basic traits in them. If they were jerks before
they had money, they are simply jerks with a billion
dollars.

Warren Buffett

Your time is limited, so don't waste it living someone
else's life.

Steve Jobs

Did you ever play the game King of the Hill when you were a kid? You would
run up a hill or a pile of dirt and proclaim, "I'm the king of the hill! Nobody
can take me!" Then your friends would charge toward you and try to push you
off the top of the hill. After all, everybody knows there's room for only one king
of the hill.

A lot of us are still playing that game as adults, but instead of wanting to
control the dirt pile, we try to control the people around us. We carry with us
an acute awareness of how much power we wield in any given relationship. The
problem is, we've got it all backward.

Jesus made a radical statement two thousand years ago that flies in the face of everything our culture teaches us. He said, "The greatest among you will be your servant. For whoever exalts himself will be humbled, and whoever humbles himself will be exalted" (Matthew 23:11–12). Like so many other truths we've looked at, what's true about pride and humility is the polar opposite of what we've grown up believing. It's not just a variation or a slight nuance of words but rather a radical and complete shift that causes us to rethink our very purpose.

Much of the stress in our lives comes from trying to gain control, because we think that if our circumstances were different, we'd finally be truly happy. We try to control our image, so we spend a lot of time managing our outward appearance. Clothes, cars, yards, and advanced degrees all require time and money. They're not bad things, but they can be a huge source of stress if you think your self-worth depends on them. We also try to control our pain. Everything from overeating to abusing alcohol and drugs can be used to try to fill the gaping wounds of our lives. Ultimately, we try to control other people, which is impossible because we can't even control our own lives.

Trying to be number one may feed your insecurities, but it will never feed your soul. You can change your outward appearance, change your wardrobe, change your job, and change your neighborhood, but *you* are still the same person. If you're an insecure, arrogant jerk on the inside, and you get a new house and a new job, unfortunately you'll still be an insecure, arrogant jerk.

On the other hand, if you're humble, caring, compassionate, and really comfortable with who God has created you to be, you'll still be humble, caring, and compassionate if you get that new job title. You see, happiness isn't determined by what's happening *outside* your life but by the choices you make *inside* your life. The Bible puts it this way: "Don't become so well-adjusted to your culture that you fit into it without even thinking. Instead, fix your attention on God. You'll be changed from the inside out" (Romans 12:2, MSG). Even when everything seems chaotic, crazy, and stressful on the outside, you can choose an attitude of peace, joy, and purpose on the inside.

Uniquely Made

The first step in letting go of pride is to stop the insanity of comparing yourself with others. God created you uniquely; you're perfectly suited for the path he has chosen for you. No one in the world has your precise physical makeup, your exact background, your combination of skills and abilities, your special relationships, or your hopes and dreams. And your spouse, kids, family, and friends—they're unique too.

Instead of creating personal and relational stress by constantly comparing yourself to others, live your own life. It's essential to break the mold by celebrating individuality—both your own and the individuality of the people you love.

Since no two marriages or parent-child relationships are alike, it's foolish to compare yours with others'. You'll always find someone who seems to have it a little better than you, and that can leave you feeling depressed and envious. And there's always someone who's in a worse situation than you are, and that can make you feel prideful. Either way, comparisons are destructive. When we spend our lives comparing, we devalue who God created us to be, wound the people we love most, and miss out on enjoying what we have.

The comparison game is dangerous and addictive, and there's only one way to stop: remember who you are in Christ.

There's a scene in Disney's *The Lion King* where Simba, the young lion who is supposed to take over his dad's role and become king, makes a life-altering decision. Simba had watched as his father was killed, and he believed it was his fault. Out of fear and guilt, he ran away and didn't assume his rightful place on the throne.

In a vision Simba's father comes to him and says, "Simba, you've forgotten me."

Simba responds, "No, Dad, I would never forget you! I love you! I miss you!"

But his father replies in a deep, booming voice, "You've forgotten who you are, therefore you've forgotten me. Simba, remember who you are. You're the one true king."

Your heavenly Father's words to you are the same. When you forget who he made you to be, you've forgotten him. It's time to stop and remember who you are—the *real* you. All of us need to be reminded. Your husband or wife needs to know that you want them to express their unique gifts and passions. Your teenager needs to hear that they're special and matter to God. Encourage them to stop imitating everyone else, because God has big plans for their life.

HUMBLE PIE

Each of us knows that deep down we're insecure and that we feel inadequate to be the kind of person we know we should be. Folks who are humble don't have a low self-esteem. They just admit to themselves and others that they feel weak and vulnerable, and they are quick to recognize that anything good they do is a result of God's grace and not their own prowess.

The concept of humility is misunderstood and unpopular. In fact, most people say you'd better look out for number one, because if you don't, no one else will. We're encouraged to be self-sufficient, self-reliant, and self-centered. But the truth is that pride will steal your happiness. Humility is the only thing that will take you from feeling stressed to being blessed.

Actually, there's a whole laundry list of reasons why I have no right to be proud: God created me, so any talents I have, he gave me in the first place. I'm depending on him for my next sunrise, my next meal, even my next breath. He could take away anything or anyone in my life at any time. In fact, when I stop to think about it, I realize that my pride is just another way of saying, "I'm not going to give God credit for this." I've discovered that the antidote to pride is acknowledging that God is the *only* certainty in my life.

The problem with pride is that it blinds us to our great need for forgiveness. I love the story Jesus tells in Luke 18 that burst the pride of self-righteous religious folks:

> Two men went to the Temple to pray. One was a proud, self-righteous Pharisee, and the other a cheating tax collector. The proud Pharisee "prayed" this prayer: "Thank God, I am not a sinner like everyone else, especially like that tax collector over there!..."
>
> But the corrupt tax collector stood at a distance and dared not even lift his eyes to heaven as he prayed, but beat upon his chest in sorrow, exclaiming, "God, be merciful to me, a sinner." I tell you, this sinner, not the Pharisee, returned home forgiven! For the proud shall be humbled, but the humble shall be honored. (verses 10–11, 13–14, TLB)

In Jesus' day tax collectors were notorious for being thieves, and the religious leaders called Pharisees were the most respected people in society. Jesus said that the religious leader looked over at the tax collector and prayed, "Thank God, I'm not like him!" while the tax collector was fully aware of his need for forgiveness.

Wow, don't you love hanging around people who are humble, thankful, and know they've been forgiven?

The next time you're having a conversation with someone you love, try focusing attention on the other person instead of thinking about what you're going to say next. Be willing to be vulnerable. Risk admitting your honest emotions, fears, and dreams. Ask questions and really try to discern what's best for the other person, even if it isn't ideal for you.

And don't worry. God has a way of taking care of your needs when you make serving others a priority. That's the key to humility. It's not looking out for number one; it's looking *up* to number One.

BREATHE

I can't be filled with my pride and God's power at the same time. It's either one or the other. Every day I'm confronted with the fact that my human love simply isn't enough to meet the needs of my spouse, my kids, or my friends. I'm too tired, too stressed, or too selfish.

That's why I come to the place each day where I realize that the pressure is too much for me and I need to take a spiritual breath. I exhale my pride, and I inhale God's power.

It's one of the greatest spiritual truths I've learned in life: when I daily admit I'm weak, God fills me with his strength. It's only when I empty myself through confession and fill up by surrendering to God's power that I'm finally able to be the spouse, parent, and friend I've always dreamed of being.

LASTING LOVE RELATIONSHIP
Challenge

1. If you're stressed out right now, it's probably because you're trying to control something that God never intended for you to handle. What situations or people do you find yourself trying to control on a regular basis?
2. In what ways do you compare yourself to others? What does that reveal about you?
3. What practical reminder could you use to prompt yourself to breathe spiritually each day and depend on God's power to love the people closest to you?

Baggage
Letting Go of Guilt

Everyone's got emotional baggage; the question is, what are
you doing to unpack that trunk and put it away, so your…
friends and relatives don't have to keep tripping over it?

SHARI SCHREIBER

Grace isn't a little prayer you chant before receiving a meal.
It's a way to live.

JACKIE WINDSPEAR

I have a picture on my desk of my daughter Megan when she was three years
old. Her back is to the camera, and she's wearing a bright pink-and-green out-
fit with a giant pink bow in her hair. Practically neon, Megan was not to be
missed even a mile away.

We were playing hide-and-seek at the time, and when it was her turn to
hide, Megan had simply run to the edge of the yard and stood right there in
the open, very still, facing a bush. No doubt she thought she was hidden. She
couldn't see anyone, so certainly no one could see her. Of course, the picture
shows how incredibly obvious she was. She stood out like brightly colored
Christmas lights on a dark night.

I love that picture because it reminds me of how I must look to God when I try to hide from him. We all know when we sin, when we blow it, when we have disobeyed God. And like Megan in that picture, we must look ridiculous to God, pretending to hide when, in fact, our guilt is flashing like a neon sign.

But what is clear to God may not be obvious to other people. Those who are close to us may not be able to detect the baggage we carry around. Likewise, we may not be able to see the guilt burdens of the people around us.

Have you ever had a conflict with someone but couldn't really put your finger on how it all started? It likely was related to past guilt and old regrets—tender places your relationship has tread on. It's like living in a room with asbestos insulation. You may not notice any symptoms right away, but over time the poison seeps in and makes everyone sick.

We all try to cover up our guilty feelings in different ways. Some try to disguise guilt by keeping up a facade of smiles. Some try to suppress it, deny it, or ignore it and pretend it doesn't exist. But however we try to cover it up, the guilt is still there, leaking through the walls.

Many don't even realize that they're carrying around a burden of guilt yet experience its devastating effects nonetheless. It comes out in anxiety, anger, and depression. It even results in illness. In fact, it's been said that more than half the people in our hospitals today could go home if they got rid of their guilt.

Because of Christ, there is a way to be free of the weight of guilt that poisons all our relationships. The Bible tells us, "He forgave all our sins. He canceled the record that contained the charges against us. He took it and destroyed it by nailing it to Christ's cross" (Colossians 2:13–14, NLT).

MERCY ME

These days the words *mercy* and *grace* get thrown about as if they're interchangeable. The truth is, they're not the same thing.

A few years back I received a traffic ticket for speeding (which I, unfortunately, deserved). The officer who stopped me handed me the ticket and said in a Texas drawl, "Now you'll need to report to Judge Justice."

Really? The judge's last name actually was Justice? I looked down and saw the address for Judge Justice neatly printed on the court paper. And without thinking, I said, "Oh, Officer, I don't want justice. I want mercy."

Mercy is when you are spared the penalty you so clearly deserve, as would have been the case if my speeding ticket had been waived (it wasn't).

Grace, on the other hand, is when you get something you don't deserve at all, like being given a gift that you didn't earn or have any right to expect. The apostle Paul explains in Ephesians 2:8–9: "For it is by grace you have been saved, through faith—and this not from yourselves, it is the gift of God—not by works, so that no one can boast." We've been given the free gift of grace. It's God's response to all my wrongs when I admit them to him.

Mercy and grace. God gives us both in our relationship with him, and that's how we know both are needed in our relationships with the people we love.

CHAINS

Let's leave behind the question of who in your key relationships is carrying around any baggage of past guilt and old regret. It could be the other person; perhaps it's you. Likely it's both of you. In either case it doesn't matter. You're both chained to it.

Over time we all tend to invent ways to deal with the awkwardness of damaged relationships, in much the same way we'd adapt to limping around with an injured foot. After a while you don't even notice you're limping. It's just the way you walk. Maybe you fall back into old patterns every time you interact with your parents, are repeatedly deceptive in conversations with your business partner, or regularly resist being forthright with your spouse. You may have used those things in the past as a crutch, and you may even know they're damaging, but you continue to use them out of habit.

The way they used to train baby elephants in the circus was to tie a chain to one of their legs and anchor the other end of the chain to the ground with a peg. The baby elephant would pull and pull against the chain, trying to break free, until he realized his efforts were futile. Finally he'd give up. The interesting thing is that the elephant would never again try to break free from the chain. Even when he was full-grown, weighed two tons, and could have easily snapped the chain and ripped the stake from the ground, he wouldn't even try. The elephant remembered, *No, this is useless. I'll always have these chains because I'm not strong enough to break them.*

To some extent we handle our relationships the same way. Just like the elephant, we continue to operate in the relational ruts of our past. The great news is that your relationships can be radically different from how they've been to this point. By extending grace to the imperfect people in our lives (and by allowing others to extend grace to us), we have the ability to overcome the "baggage of before."

BAGGAGE DROP

Transformation begins with acknowledging that *we* personally need God's grace. It's important to start here, because we can't give what we haven't received. We're then set free to see our relationships with new eyes and recognize the huge potential for change.

The next step is to identify the particular chains or old patterns that affect each of your key relationships. Sometimes we're so close to our problems that we can't see clearly enough to think rationally. If that's you, I encourage you to invite someone you trust to meet you for coffee and ask them to be a mirror to you, to help you see where you could make healthy changes in the ways you relate to the people you love.

After you isolate the cause, it's time to break the chains. Try to condense into just a sentence or two what you want your relationship to look like. For instance, "I want to bring total honesty, integrity, and transparency to my marriage." Focusing on what you want things to be like is a lot more effective than fixating on what's wrong. Set your goal, and give everything you've got to fulfilling it.

Keep in mind that as much as we'd like to, we can't control how the other person will respond. They might continue to relate to you the way they always have or feel threatened by the new you. Don't worry. That's normal. Very possibly, as you change your patterns and let go of your baggage, they'll be motivated to do the same. Change in one person is often a catalyst for change in the other. Just continue to be consistent in your words and actions, and chances are, pretty soon the people around you will begin to act differently too. And if they don't?

That's what grace is for.

LASTING LOVE RELATIONSHIP
Challenge

1. What past personal failure are you having a hard time forgetting? Add this verse to your journal: "Forget the former things; do not dwell on the past" (Isaiah 43:18).
2. Chains are the old patterns we continue to use in relationships even though the need for them no longer exists. What are the chains in some of your key relationships?
3. Do you sense that someone you're close to is burdened by past guilt? Sometimes sharing our own guilt and regret gives the people we love the courage to do the same. Log on to onemonthtolove.com for more help in letting go of guilt.

Improving Your Serve

Letting Go of Selfishness

> A red rose is not selfish because it wants to be a red
> rose. It would be horribly selfish if it wanted all the
> other flowers in the garden to be both red and roses.
> OSCAR WILDE

> I don't know what your destiny will be, but one thing I
> do know: the only ones among you who will be really
> happy are those who have sought and found how to serve.
> ALBERT SCHWEITZER

When our son Josh was a preschooler, he had a friend over to play for the first time. It didn't take but a few minutes before we heard an awful scream from his room. I frantically rushed in to find Josh's red cheeks soaked with tears. Alarmed, I asked, "What happened? Are you hurt?"

He pointed to his friend and through tears exclaimed, "He's playing with my toys!"

"That's the point of having a friend over," I told him. "You just need to learn to share."

He then verbalized what most of us feel: "But I don't want to share!"

"Josh, welcome to the human race," I said. "At first no one wants to share, but after you do, it makes you feel good." He didn't buy it at the moment, but things calmed down eventually as Josh sucked it up and reluctantly started sharing.

Love at first sight is really very much about *me*. "He likes me!" "She likes me!" "If only she'd go out with me, then I'd be popular."

Lasting love redirects our focus to others, not for our ultimate benefit, but simply for theirs. To reach true lasting love relationships, we need to learn to live unselfishly. We must let go of *me*.

THE ULTIMATE EXAMPLE

Remember in the Bible when the disciples met in the Upper Room the night before Christ died? Jesus did something that night that shocked them. He washed their feet.

To us today, foot washing sounds like a strange practice. Back then, however, it was a common and necessary part of the daily routine. After a long day of walking on dusty streets in sandals, feet were filthy and caked with dirt. Although foot washing was a necessary practice, it was certainly an unpleasant one. That's why it was always delegated to the lowest servant.

Around the table that night, someone needed to wash everyone's feet, but no one wanted to be compared to a lowly servant. In fact, it was common for the disciples to argue over which of them was the greatest. As the disciples looked around the table, no doubt wondering who would be the lowest-ranking one to whom the task would fall, Jesus himself knelt down with the basin and towel. *The Son of God himself washed their feet.*

In doing so, Jesus redefined greatness. He visually made the point that greatness is about serving. He demonstrated that loving relationships are about letting go of *me* and serving others.

If I want to have a truly great marriage, I must learn to serve my spouse. If I want to be a truly great parent, I must learn to unselfishly serve my family. If

I want deep and meaningful friendships, I must learn to take *myself* out of the picture and serve my friends.

KEEPING SCORE

Do you have a tendency to keep score in your key relationships? That is, do you think, *Because I've done this or that for them, it's time for them to match my effort?* I think we all do that to some extent. It's certainly common in close relationships. But when we keep score, we hold on to *me*. We're trying to make sure we don't get shafted or taken advantage of. *What if I serve them and they don't serve me back? What if I meet their needs but they don't even attempt to meet mine?*

Unfortunately, we all encounter some relationships that are not mutual, such as friends or family who don't reciprocate by giving back. It's important to honestly share your feelings with others when your needs aren't being met. It's essential to express your anger and frustration. You shouldn't be a doormat that gets walked on all the time or develop a martyr complex. That's not healthy for the relationship either. Relationships that don't give back at all aren't real relationships. It's appropriate to deal with those special cases in their own way.

But most of the time, true working relationships aren't so one-sided. Still, we keep score anyway, essentially saying, "*I* am the most important person here, and *I* need to make sure *I'm* getting *my* proper due." That kind of attitude immediately separates people, maybe in ways that are subtle in the moment but strongly felt later on. It's like two children sharing a bedroom and dividing their stuff in a neat line right down the middle of the room. We're saying, "I'm protecting me."

To have a breakthrough in a relationship, I have to stop keeping score. I have to let go of *me* so I can embrace Christ's example of serving. After Christ washed the disciples' feet, he gave us these instructions: "Now that I, your Lord and Teacher, have washed your feet, you also should wash one another's feet" (John 13:14). Jesus modeled for us the power of serving, and then he challenged us to let go and wholeheartedly serve the people in our lives.

WHO'S IN ORBIT?

It's interesting to take the measure of our relationships and honestly assess if we frequently seek to put ourselves at the center of them.

For nearly two thousand years of human history, it was widely believed that the universe revolved around Earth. The assumption was that planet Earth was unique and the center of everything. Likewise it was assumed that we as humans were important, so the universe certainly must revolve around us.

It took Polish astronomer Nicolaus Copernicus in the early 1500s to dare to say that the Earth revolves around the sun. What Copernicus had discovered wasn't well received. In fact, it was criticized by people in science as well as in the church. In time his findings were proven true, and the Copernican revolution took hold.

In many ways this is the same revolution we need in our lives and relationships. We need the *aha!* of realizing that we aren't the center of another person's universe. Only then will we finally let go and embrace a life that revolves around service.

REDEFINING GREATNESS

John Wooden won ten NCAA basketball championships as coach of the UCLA Bruins in the sixties and seventies and is considered one of the greatest coaches of all time. To his former players and peers, he was also known as one of the greatest servant leaders of all time. Several years ago sportswriter Rick Reilly described Wooden this way:

> ...loyal to one woman, one school, one way; walking around campus in his sensible shoes and Jimmy Stewart morals....
>
> Coach would say, "Never lie, never cheat, never steal...earn the right to be proud and confident."...

He believed in hopelessly out-of-date stuff that never did anything but win championships.[12]

His legendary coaching skills, however, paled in comparison to his timeless relational gifts. Coach Wooden was married to his wife, Nellie, for fifty-three years. After her death in 1985, he continued to honor her memory and celebrate the life they shared by writing his sweetheart a letter every month. After pouring his heart out on paper, Coach Wooden carefully added to the pile of letters stacked on Nellie's pillow. He continued to exemplify lasting love, even as he waited to see his precious wife again—a reunion that took place in 2010.

How did he do it? He redefined our culture's definition of greatness by deciding that his beliefs were more important than basketball. He said, "I have always tried to make it clear that basketball is not the ultimate. It is of small importance in comparison to the total life we live. There is only one kind of life that truly wins, and that is the one that places faith in the hands of the Savior."[13]

By serving others, you redefine yourself and create a transformative atmosphere around you. We started Woodlands Church seventeen years ago with just fifteen people. By what can only be described as God's grace, it grew rapidly into a large church. After a few years I realized that many people in the community who had never attended had started using the phrase "that big church" to describe us. We wanted the people who had never attended our church to see in us Christ's attitude of serving, regardless of how many people attended.

So we started something that changed the perception of many of those who had never attended our church. More important, it changed us. For one month every year we do something we call "the Ripple Effect," mobilizing our church to go out into the community to perform acts of service. We do everything from raking leaves and mowing yards to washing cars, cleaning garages, and pumping gas.

Our goal is to touch everyone in our community with an act of service without expecting anything in return. When we finish an act of service for someone, we hand them a little Ripple Effect card that has the church's name and this quote: "What we do here today will echo into eternity." We tell them the reason we wanted to serve them was to show that we care and that Christ loves them. We never take money for our service, and we never try to get them to come to our church. There are no strings attached. We just want people to experience the power of serving. Then we encourage them to create a ripple effect by serving someone else in their life.

It's been amazing to watch as what started out as a small ripple in the pond has now created waves that are impacting our community and beyond.

When Jesus knelt to wash his disciples' feet, he redefined what it means to be in a loving relationship. Servanthood transforms us in a dramatic way. If you really want to transform your key relationships, let go of selfishness and pick up the towel of servanthood.

LASTING LOVE RELATIONSHIP
Challenge

1. When it comes to serving, are you keeping score in any of your key relationships?
2. Jesus took the first step to stop the scorekeeping among his disciples by humbly washing their feet. What action can you take that would serve others and help you let go of *me*?
3. Ask God to give you the power to go a whole week serving others without worrying whether anyone else is serving you. Journal about your experience as you go.
4. Go to onemonthtolove.com, and find out how you can start the Ripple Effect.

Ever After

Letting Go of Unrealistic Expectations

You know you're in love when you can't fall asleep
because reality is finally better than your dreams.
           DR. SEUSS

There are some people who live in a dream world,
and there are some who face reality; and then there
are those who turn one into the other.
           DOUGLAS H. EVERETT

I had a friend in college who had what he called "the list." It was the thirty things he was looking for in a wife. It included everything from the color of her eyes to her musical ability.

Sometimes he would get really frustrated because it was so hard to find a girl who met even five or six of the criteria on his list. Finally I told him, "Don't worry, because if you ever find the perfect girl who matches all thirty characteristics on your list, *you* won't be on her list." He eventually threw it away, and today he's happily married to a wonderful and—thankfully—imperfect woman.

Most people enter marriage with unspoken expectations. It can be anything from an expectation about financial decisions to an assumption about where they'll eat dinner. When expectations aren't met, they're left disappointed and discouraged.

I remember the first time we had an argument after we were married. It really scared us. We had this unrealistic image that the perfect couple never argues and lives happily ever after. We immediately thought, *Wow. We just got really mad at each other. What's wrong with our marriage?* Of course, now we know that our initial image of marriage wasn't only unrealistic but impossible! The best marriages aren't those without conflict. The best marriages are those that realize conflict is inevitable and essential to growing deeper.

Even more destructive than the fantasy of a perfect marriage is the fantasy that you are in a relationship with a perfect person. Drs. Les and Leslie Parrott state, "Bad things happen to good marriages when we expect our partner to think, feel, and behave the way we want them to—and we won't change those expectations even over time."[14]

Almost everyone has gone into a relationship thinking, *I've found the perfect person,* but it doesn't take long to discover how wrong we were. J. Grant Howard says, "We have a picture of the perfect partner, but we marry an imperfect person. Then we have two options. Tear up the picture and accept the person or tear up the person and accept the picture."

I'm afraid many couples choose to keep accepting a fantasy and tear up the beautiful reality they could have had together.

This actually applies to all relationships. As we've already mentioned, many parents have a mental picture of what they want their kids to be like, act like, and look like. When parents unsuccessfully try to make the child they *have* match the child of their *dreams,* the child's self-esteem is destroyed.

Best friends, too, can suffer from "great expectations." A friendship we previously had can unrealistically color our expectations for a new friend. Our crazy ideas of what the perfect friend would be like sets up our real-life friends for failure. When our friend isn't up to that daunting job description we've created for them, we assume something must be terribly wrong with them.

Love at first sight easily falls into the trap of unrealistic expectations. We all enjoy stories about the guy and girl whose eyes meet "across a crowded room" and the Cinderella fairy tales of the peasant girl finding her prince. But that's not real life.

Lasting love says that beautiful relationships grow from the soil of reality—a truthful understanding of someone else's strengths *and* weaknesses. It's time to let go of the perfect picture of the people closest to us and embrace the reality that none of us is perfect.

Your Key Relationships—Works of Art

The first time we went to the Louvre in Paris, we headed straight for Leonardo da Vinci's sixteenth-century oil painting of the woman with the enigmatic smile: *Mona Lisa.*

I have to be honest. When I first saw the *Mona Lisa,* I thought, *What's the big deal?* The painting just wasn't what I'd expected. First, it was smaller than I had imagined. It's only thirty inches by twenty inches. Second, the woman in the painting was just as plain and ordinary and unexciting as she is in all the inexpensive reproductions I've seen through the years. How could something that appears plain and ordinary at first glance command even a second look?

Well, I just revealed how much I know about art, because the *Mona Lisa* is the most valuable masterpiece in the world. It's owned by the French government, yet it's uninsured because it's priceless. At first glance the untrained eye just doesn't see the value of the *Mona Lisa.*

This reminds me of how we often see the people we are closest to. It's easy to look past their great value and see only their imperfections. The reality is that you and the people you love are priceless works of art. The Bible says, "For we are God's masterpiece. He has created us anew in Christ Jesus, so that we can do the good things he planned for us long ago" (Ephesians 2:10, NLT).

The people you love are priceless works of art, not perfect works of art. Lasting love means that you appreciate the masterpieces God has placed in your life.

Appreciation literally means "to raise in value." The *Mona Lisa* has been appreciated by so many people over the years that its value is beyond any price. When I constantly appreciate the people in my life, it raises their value. Ultimately, they are, as the MasterCard commercials say, "priceless."

I appreciate the people in my life when I start to accept them and stop trying to change them. Now, I'm not saying they don't need to change. They may have a lot of areas in their life where they need to make changes. The problem is that nagging, criticizing, and negativism will never do the trick. Much as you try to bend others into your ideal expectations of them, they'll fall short. Much as you try, you can't change another person. You can only change yourself with God's help and power in your life.

When I start accepting the people I love, it provides an atmosphere where change can take place. When you accept someone, it doesn't mean you approve of their behavior. It doesn't mean you agree with everything they do. It doesn't mean you condone all their weaknesses. It *does* mean that you see them as a masterpiece created by God, despite their imperfections.

BUCKET LIST

Tom Rath and Donald Clifton say that we experience approximately twenty thousand interactive moments every day. Some of those interactive moments are positive, some of them are negative, and some are neutral.

Rath and Clifton say that everyone has an "invisible bucket." The positive interactions fill up our buckets, and the negative ones drain our buckets. We are at our best when our buckets are overflowing, and we are at our worst when our buckets are empty and there is nothing left to give.[15]

Reinforcing this theory, John Gottman did a study on marriage by rating the positive and negative interactions a couple experiences. He found that marriages with a positive-negative interaction ratio of five-to-one (that is five positive interactions to one negative interaction) are significantly healthier than those whose negative ratios are higher. In fact, he says that he can predict with greater than 90 percent accuracy whether a marriage will make it, based on this positive-negative interaction ratio.

The point is, choose to fill up the buckets of the people closest to you with words and actions of appreciation. When you start filling their buckets, yours will be filled to overflowing.

LOST OPPORTUNITIES

I found this really interesting. In 1911 the *Mona Lisa* was stolen from the Louvre. The painting was gone for two years before they recovered it in 1913. The amazing thing is that during those two years more people came to see the blank wall in the museum where the painting had hung than had come in the two years before it was stolen.

As is often the case, it was appreciated more after it was gone. Lasting love is not only about appreciating someone's value but also about being aware of how brief our time is with them. Discovering how we can love someone more the next time we're with them than the last time is so important, especially as we realize that the last time we are with someone might really be the last...*forever.* When that time comes, what will we wish we had said or done?

There are people in your life you need to appreciate today. Don't wait until they're gone. Don't wait until it's too late. Don't wait for a fantasy and fail to appreciate your reality.

The Bible says, "Therefore, as we have opportunity, let us do good to all people" (Galatians 6:10). God has given you some opportunities today to appreciate the people you love. Take advantage of them.

LASTING LOVE RELATIONSHIP
Challenge

1. Do you carry a mental picture of what you expect the people you love to be like and act like? Tear up the picture in your mind, and make a list of the character qualities you want to exhibit in your own life.

2. Write down three things you appreciate about three key people in your life. Find a time to tell them how much you value them, and share with them the specific things you appreciate most about them.

3. How full is your bucket right now? Ask God to give you the strength to express appreciation even if you don't feel you have anything to give right now. And ask him to fill you up with encouragement as you encourage others.

Illuminate

Letting Go of Shadows

> Those who love deeply never grow old; they may die
> of old age, but they die young.
>
> SIR ARTHUR WING PINERO

> If we never met again in our lives, I should feel that
> somehow the whole adventure of existence was justi-
> fied by my having met you.
>
> LEWIS MUMFORD, TO HIS WIFE

As the director of the Space Telescope Science Institute in Baltimore, Mary-land, Dr. Robert Williams was given the opportunity to have ten days' access to the Hubble, America's most famous space telescope. Enormous, expensive telescopes are generally used to mine data for large projects and are managed by a collaboration between countries or universities, so this was an incredible opportunity for an astrophysicist.

Williams made a surprising decision during his short time with the Hub-ble. Instead of training the lens on any of a number of critical projects, he turned it toward a small patch of black sky. And he left it pointed there for ten days in 1995.

The result was the amazingly detailed image called the Hubble Deep Field. In this incredibly small area, where only a few stars of the Milky Way were previously known to exist, the Hubble revealed a bewildering thirteen thousand galaxies.[16] The depth and breadth of creation this image revealed was truly humbling on a universal scale. What was thought to be empty space just needed a lot of light focused on it to reveal its true potential.

The dark places in our relationships are just the same. After all, darkness is just the absence of light. The great news is that you were never intended to live in the dark. Jesus Christ has "called you out of darkness into his wonderful light" (1 Peter 2:9). He wants to illuminate your closest relationships and fill those empty, aching places in your heart.

Have you been unfaithful to your marriage partner? He will give you the strength for commitment. Do you feel insecure in a friendship? He will fill you with trust. Are you struggling with your teenager? He will enable you to communicate honestly and openly. Are you lonely? He will help you to have meaningful connections. When his light shines into the darkest corners of your relationships, you'll see an incredible potential for love that you never even knew existed.

NEARSIGHTED

Throughout this book we've encouraged you to take another look at what you've assumed to be true about relationships. This new way of seeing the people you love the most can become a lifestyle if you just remember that there's a lot more to relationships than what you see—and do—on the surface.

When I was seven years old, my second grade class was given a vision test at school, which I failed miserably. My mom took me to the local optometrist, who confirmed that my eyesight was something south of 20/400. A couple of weeks later we returned to his office to pick up my new Coke-bottle-thick, wire-rimmed glasses. This was the seventies, and since I already wore headgear to correct an overbite, my look was now complete. I remember everything about that afternoon, even the smell of the tiny bottle of purple cleaner the assistant used as she carefully sprayed and wiped my new glasses before she handed them to me. I was really excited, mostly because of the fashion statement I was sure to make with my new look. As far as seeing went, I just didn't get what all the fuss was about.

When the assistant facing me across the counter finally slid my new glasses on my nose, my mouth literally dropped open. Maybe for the first time since I'd learned to talk, I had no words for what I was experiencing. Everything in the room had instantaneously come into sharp focus. Until that moment I had lived in a bubble, always focused on what was happening within arm's length; the rest of the world had been blurry and indistinct. Now my world had suddenly exploded in depth and detail.

Speechless, I shoved open the swinging door with the tinkling bell, leaped onto the sidewalk, and simply stared. The trees—they had bazillions of leaves! And each leaf was turning and blowing individually. Birds were flying, and (I couldn't believe this) they were actually making a letter *V* like in the cartoons. And the roofs of the houses—they were made up of little tiny squares like a quilt.

I hung my head out the window of our wood-sided station wagon the whole way home, absolutely awestruck at the incredible world I'd just discovered.

After my grand transformation, I remember my parents and teachers asking me, "Why didn't you tell us you couldn't see?" Well, that thought had never occurred to me. It had never once crossed my mind that what I saw was different from what anyone else saw. I assumed that everyone was like me, seeing clearly what was up close and everything beyond blurring together like melted crayons.

Most of us are naturally nearsighted when it comes to relationships. It's easy to get discouraged when we see our daily struggles in sharp detail but see only a hazy big picture of where we're headed. As we trudge through our lives staring at our muddy feet instead of keeping our eyes on the horizon, we become trapped in a bubble of fear and anxiety. We focus on the deep needs of the people we love and our own inability to address them, and we begin to believe that what we can see is all there is.

The truth is just the opposite. What we *can't* see is far more real than what we *can* see. That's why clear vision is the key to hope. Scripture tells us, "So we fix our eyes not on what is seen, but on what is unseen. For what is seen is temporary, but what is unseen is eternal" (2 Corinthians 4:18). Our narrow view of love and life explodes with meaning when we see through God's eyes.

FACE TO FACE

Our last sight on earth will intersect with our first sight of heaven. That's the moment I'm waiting for! You see, as a kid when I put on my glasses for the first time, the *world* didn't change—*I* did. I could finally see things as they had been all along. So it will be with us. The apostle Paul describes it this way: "Now we see but a poor reflection as in a mirror; then we shall see face to face. Now I know in part; then I shall know fully, even as I am fully known" (1 Corinthians 13:12).

Did you catch that? We were created to be fully known. That explains why every person on the planet aches to be completely understood, accepted, and loved. It's what we were made for. That's why we are willing to risk pain, humiliation, and rejection even when the odds are against us. It's why we forgive when we've been deeply wounded time and time again. And it's why we keep on giving even when we're certain to get nothing in return. We were created in the image of God, and he is love (see 1 John 4:16). That's what makes us human: our insatiable desire to love and be loved.

Because we live in an imperfect and broken world, there will be times in our relationships when it's hard to see what God is up to. There are seasons when it's difficult to see that God is making something beautiful out of the brokenness. That's because here on earth we see a "poor reflection" of what real love is.

One day, however, we will see love clearly and fully because we shall see "face to face." When we finally look into the face of the One who created us and gave his life for us, we will see reflected in his eyes lasting love.

Until then, get face to face with the people in your life with the goal being that the next time you're together, you will grow closer than you were the time before. The next time you're face to face with someone you love, ask yourself, If this were the last time we were together on earth, what would I say, and what would I do? Then say it now. Share it now. Love now!

We encourage you to make the Lasting Love Relationship Challenge a way of living. Every one of the relational arts we've begun to practice is like any artistic endeavor. To become great will take a lifetime of practice.

The highest goal we can have this side of heaven is to love like Christ. You've now begun your lifelong journey of growing and developing rich, meaningful relationships. Continue to do whatever it takes to live a life of love. If you do, your last sight on earth is sure to be your best. And your first sight of heaven? There will be no words…

"No eye has seen, no ear has heard, no mind has conceived what God has prepared for those who love him" (1 Corinthians 2:9).

LASTING LOVE RELATIONSHIP
Challenge

1. What has happened in your key relationships this month? Have you seen things with more clarity than you did before?

2. Do you sense that things have gotten unstuck, something has deepened, or a problem has been solved? In your journal write some impressions of what has changed for you over the past thirty days.

3. Relationships are an ongoing work of the heart. What might you do in your relationships with the people you love most to keep them growing and strengthening in the days to come? What other relationships in your life might you focus on next? Log on to onemonthtolove.com, and discover how to turn the Lasting Love Relationship Challenge into a lifestyle.

One Month to Love
Relationship Summary and Index

We have primarily discussed three types of relationships in this book: friendships, marriage, and parenting. For quick reference, we've included the following index to specific nuggets of advice or information in those three categories.

Keep in mind, however, that many of the principles and strategies we discuss throughout the book can be applied to any relationship, whether it's with your spouse, children, friends, parents, or siblings.

FRIEND RELATIONSHIPS

Page

56   Being there for someone in the hard times of life usually is inconven-
       ient and difficult and requires sacrifice. But often it also becomes its
       own reward, a privilege that gives back to us in unexpected ways.

100–1 If you want a friendship to go to a deeper level, you must feel free to
       tell each other when you disagree or don't like the direction the other
       person is going.

107–8 If someone you love is stuck in a place where they're confused, frus-
       trated, and restless, simply understanding more about their phase of
       life can be a big help.

111   A few well-timed words of encouragement to a friend can make the
       difference between someone giving up on their dream or deciding to
       persevere.

114   Encouragement is one person being vulnerable and allowing another
       to enter into their private world and that person respecting that inner
       sanctum and speaking into it, helping to challenge the fear that re-
       sides there.

115   If you really love someone, you don't focus on "Why didn't that
       happen to me?" or "Why are they blessed and I'm not?" Instead, you
       will be the one who plans the celebration and throws the confetti.

122   We sometimes feel awkward even in close relationships, and we have to
       realize that the other person may feel awkward too. But we need to take
       responsibility in furthering and deepening the relationship by sacrificing
       our own comfort, overcoming our fears, and risking awkwardness.

124   Even the best relationships have rough edges, difficult moments, and
       embarrassing confessions. It takes a commitment to risk, a willingness
       to be uncomfortable at times, and real action if you want to see a
       transformation in your key relationships.

128   Friends become distant when they make false assumptions and stop
       trying to learn more about each other.

MARRIAGE RELATIONSHIPS

Page

69   Every relationship has unique challenges, and how you respond in the hard times determines whether you will walk off the dance floor in the middle of the song or discover the divine dance of lasting love.

80   The very act of creating and sharing a vision for your marriage will strengthen it.

86   Don't wait for your spouse to make the first move. You be the blessing. Strive to outlove and outgive each other.

93   Schedule your life calendar around your relationship rather than the other way around.

98   If you really want to solve your relationship problems and experience lasting love, you have to be willing to get beyond the petty surface issues and intentionally go to a deeper level.

100   Some spouses always try to win the argument, and in the process they lose the relationship.

128   In marriage we may mistakenly think that our spouse's needs are the same as our own, and in so doing, we completely skip over the crucial questions that take relationships to the deepest level.

136   If we want to move past shallow, superficial relationships into the deep, connected, rich relationships God wants for us, we have to let go of the opinions of others and be willing to expose our true selves.

145   Many couples say, "We just don't have feelings for each other anymore." The big mistake they make is waiting for the loving feelings to come back before they start acting in loving ways.

153   Often something trivial sparks anger, yet the real reason for the anger may be found days, months, or even years deeper.

167   Couples are better together because no one has every strength; everyone has many weaknesses.

PARENTING RELATIONSHIPS

Page

48   Commitment means that you won't check out when your kids disap-
      point you; you'll stay engaged in their lives no matter what.

49   Your job as a parent is to work yourself out of a job.

86   The smallest intentional action step—like eating lunch together in
      the school cafeteria—can make all the difference in your relationship
      with your child.

87   If you want to connect with your teenagers, you have to look for ways
      to step into their world.

112   As parents, we need to deal with our own issues without saddling our
      kids with the responsibility of fulfilling our lost dreams.

120   When we, as parents, act as if we never have any problems, it makes
      our kids feel as though they can't share their failures and struggles
      with us because we wouldn't be able to relate.

128   Many parents really love their teenagers, but the teens don't feel loved,
      because the parents aren't expressing love in a way their children can
      receive it.

195   Each parent-child relationship is unique, and it is destructive to make
      comparisons. When we spend our lives comparing, we devalue who
      God created us to be, wound the people we love most, and fail to
      enjoy what we have.

196   Teenagers need to hear that they are special and matter to God. En-
      courage them to stop imitating everyone else, because God has big
      plans for their life.

206   If we want to be truly great parents, we must learn to unselfishly serve
      our families.

Notes

1. Helen Colton, *The Gift of Touch: How Physical Contact Improves Communication, Pleasure, and Health* (New York: Seaview/Putnam, 1983), 49, quoted in Gary Smalley and John Trent, *The Blessing* (New York: Pocket Books/Simon and Shuster, 1990), 48.

2. T. D. Jakes, *Woman, Thou Art Loosed! Healing the Wounds of the Past* (Shippensburg, PA: Destiny Image, 1993), 115.

3. Erma Bombeck, "No More Oatmeal Kisses," © Newsday Inc., 1969, quoted in Jack Canfield and others, *Chicken Soup for the Mother's Soul: 101 Stories to Open the Hearts and Rekindle the Spirits of Mothers* (Deerfield Beach, FL: Health Communications, 1997), 133.

4. The wording is from the 2004 edition.

5. Margery Williams, *The Velveteen Rabbit* (Philadelphia: Running Press, 1997), 10, 12–13.

6. Lawrence J. Crabb Jr. and Dan B. Allender, *Encouragement: The Key to Caring* (Grand Rapids: Zondervan, 1984), 32.

7. Marilyn Elias, "Uplift in Good Times Shows Happy Couples," *USA Today*, June 17, 2009, www.usatoday.com/news/nation/2009-06-17-happy-couples_N.htm.

8. Debra Fine, *The Fine Art of Small Talk: How to Start a Conversation, Keep It Going, Build Networking Skills—and Leave a Positive Impression* (New York: Hyperion, 2005), 20.

9. Michael Reagan with Jim Denney, *Twice Adopted* (Nashville: Broadman and Holman, 2004), xvi.

10. John Eldredge, *Wild at Heart: Discovering the Passionate Soul of a Man* (Nashville: Thomas Nelson, 2001), 52.

11. Beth Moore, *So Long, Insecurity: You've Been a Bad Friend to Us* (Carol Stream, IL: Tyndale, 2010), 15.

12. Rick Reilly, "A Paragon Rising Above the Madness," *Sports Illustrated*, March 14, 2000, http://sportsillustrated.cnn.com/inside_game/ magazine/life_of_reilly/news/2000/03/14/life_of_reilly.

13. John R. Wooden with Jack Tobin, *They Call Me Coach* (New York: McGraw-Hill, 2004), 95.

14. Les Parrott and Leslie Parrott, *When Bad Things Happen to Good Marriages: How to Stay Together When Life Pulls You Apart* (Grand Rapids: Zondervan, 2001), 35.

15. Tom Rath and Donald O. Clifton, *How Full Is Your Bucket? Positive Strategies for Work and Life* (New York: Gallup Press, 2004), 25.

16. "The Future of Astronomy: Black-Sky Thinking," *The Economist*, August 13, 2009.